"Larry Crabb has done it again! In *A Different Kind of Happiness* I've been diagnosed gently, kindly shown Jesus, and then offered a better way. This is a profound, honest, life-changing book. This old cynical preacher found hope here. You will too. Love changes everything, but it's love that is more than a cliché. This is real love that stands up and sings the Hallelujah Chorus."

Steve Brown, radio broadcaster, author, and seminary professor

"Dr. Larry Crabb has a unique mind, and this book demonstrates this from start to finish. You will not be able to put this book down. Dr. Crabb shows the way to true happiness and joy—being like Jesus and getting your joy from Him. This is a book that will make you think, and you may never be quite the same again after reading it."

R. T. Kendall, former minister of Westminster Chapel, London (1977–2002)

"It is no exaggeration that Dr. Crabb has had a profound impact upon me, my family, and the community of believers to which I belong. Like his favorite prophet, Jeremiah, Dr. Crabb has a message that challenges the status quo: ultimately the Bible is about relationship. His latest book is a welcome yet challenging call to a lived relational theology. He reminds us that growing in sacrificial other-centeredness is not easy but it is the way of Christ, which is a critical message for the body of Christ."

Jason Kanz, PhD, ABPP, board certified in clinical neuropsychology, Marshfield Clinic

"For *any* Christian seriously committed to living as Jesus lived and loving as Jesus loved, this book is *required* reading. Functioning like a spiritual MRI, it exposes the narratives that support our flawed quest for happiness and resultant failure to love well. A diagnosis like this is not comfortable but it is required if we are to cooperate with the Spirit in the renovation of our hearts, to enjoy God as our greatest good, and to display His life in the way we relate to others."

Dr. Miriam Dixon, pastor, First Presbyterian Church, Golden, Colorado

"While reading this book I found my heart longing to love like Jesus loves. Larry writes in a way that stirs the deepest part of me, which truly does want what God wants. I wish every Christ-follower would read this book and allow God to create a vision in them for loving well. As a pastor I long to see this kind of Christlike loving lived out in and through every local church. If we did, the world would know that Jesus was sent from the Father and that we are *His*. Happy reading."

Bill Lenz, senior pastor, Christ the Rock Community Church, Appleton, Wisconsin

"It's time perhaps to recapture a bit of John Calvin's wisdom. He wrote that true wisdom is the product of two necessities: knowledge of God and knowledge of oneself. As usual, Dr. Crabb calls the reader to an awareness of oneself that opens the door for the truths of God to actually impact how one relates. For the honest pilgrim, it is an uncomfortable process, but as King Solomon wisely observed, the road to life most often travels through what seems like death (Prov. 14:12). We were built for happiness. The path there is mostly misidentified and counterintuitive. In this book, Larry points to the life-giving way. And he does so with a comprehensive

© 2016 by Larry Crabb

Published by Baker Books
a division of Baker Publishing Group
P.O. Box 6287, Grand Rapids, MI 49516-6287
www.bakerbooks.com

Printed in the United States of America

Library of Congress Cataloging-in-Publication Data
Names: Crabb, Larry, 1944– author.
Title: A different kind of happiness : discovering the joy that comes from sacrificial love / Dr. Larry Crabb.
Description: Grand Rapids : Baker Books, 2016. | Includes bibliographical references.
Identifiers: LCCN 2015047248 | ISBN 9780801015311 (cloth) | ISBN 9780801015342
Subjects: LCSH: Joy—Religious aspects—Christianity. | Happiness—Religious aspects—Christianity. | Love—Religious aspects—Christianity. | Sacrifice—Christianity.
Classification: LCC BV4647.J68 C58 2016 | DDC 248.4—dc23
LC record available at http://lccn.loc.gov/2015047248

Unless otherwise indicated, Scripture quotations are from the *Holy Bible*, New Living Translation, copyright © 1996, 2004, 2007 by Tyndale House Foundation. Used by permission of Tyndale House Publishers, Inc., Carol Stream, Illinois 60188. All rights reserved.

Scripture quotations labeled ESV are from The Holy Bible, English Standard Version® (ESV®), copyright © 2001 by Crossway, a publishing ministry of Good News Publishers. Used by permission. All rights reserved. ESV Text Edition: 2011

Scripture quotations labeled MSG are from *The Message* by Eugene H. Peterson, copyright © 1993, 1994, 1995, 2000, 2001, 2002. Used by permission of NavPress Publishing Group. All rights reserved.

Emphasis in Scripture quotations has been added by the author.

Some names and details have been changed to protect the privacy of those who have shared their stories with the author.

16 17 18 19 20 21 22   7 6 5 4 3 2 1

To the nearly two thousand friends who have participated in the School of Spiritual Direction and to Trip, Kent, Karla, Paul, Maribeth, Tom, and Anthony, who have served as spiritual directors; your lives have touched mine. I'm grateful.

To my sisters and brothers at First Presbyterian Church of Golden, Colorado, a spiritually forming community that reveals God's love to Rachael and to me; and to Dr. Miriam (Mimi) Dixon, who shepherds our community, and me, with the love and wisdom she receives from Jesus.

To Tom and Jenny, Bob and Claudia: our more than a decade long journey together on the narrow road has provided Rachael and me with uncommon encouragement. Close long-term friends are a rare gift.

Contents

Acknowledgments

My name is on the cover of this publication, but no book is the product of one person. I couldn't possibly list the name of every person, living or dead, who has shaped my thinking and strengthened me in the long process of writing. A short list will have to do.

Sincere thanks to:

- Chad Allen, Lindsey Spoolstra, and the supportive team at Baker Books. Chad and Lindsey, your thoughtful editing has vastly improved this manuscript.
- Five close pastor friends: Trip Moore (a freelance pastor in Belgium), Kent Denlinger, Jim Kallam, Bill Lenz, and Jamie Rasmussen. Your perseverance in your call has energized me to persevere in mine.
- Dr. James Houston, Dr. J. I. Packer, and Jerry Miller: through brief conversations over many years each of you has meaningfully mentored me far more than you realize.
- Butch and Arlita: it's strangely wonderful how providence has woven our lives together. Keep following your dreams. They're from the Lord. I'm looking forward to a cup of coffee and a conversation that matters at the Red Dot Coffee House.

- Kep, Kimmie, Ken, Lesley, Josie, Jake, Kaitlyn, Keira, and Kenzie: two sons, two daughters-in-law, five grandchildren— family reaches places in my heart nothing else can. Your patience with a too-often-preoccupied father and grandfather is a gift of grace to me.

- Rich and Karlene: rarely have I been blessed with such faithfully guiding and supportive friends. Your vision for what God longs to do keeps my eyes focused up.

- Some clichés actually mean something. This one does. Last but not least, to our "little team" that keeps New Way Ministries moving:

    Andi: we wouldn't be as alive and blessed without you. You're terrific!

    Kep: I couldn't be more proud as your father or more grateful as your employer. You're extraordinary!

    Rachael: when we said our vows, had I known what would unfold over fifty years of marriage, I'd have fallen to my knees in worship. You're more than everything a husband could want! I love you.

Prologue

If it's true, as the once popular song declared, that "Love makes the world go 'round," then we have reason to ask a disturbing question: *Is the worst problem in the world a shortfall of love?* Just about everywhere, from terrorist threats to political corruption, from school shootings to troubled marriages, the world gives evidence that love is in limited supply.

In the song, I assume *world* refers to human culture, to the world of people that functions well only to the degree that people function well, relationally. Other spheres of life and culture, such as movie-making, art displays, medical research, technology development, and perhaps even church activities, seem able to move along quite nicely without anyone having to relate at a deeply personal level. Human competence and commitment, as well as effective communication and sensitive congeniality, are required for success in those kinds of endeavors. Human connecting, the soul-to-soul relating that only Jesus makes possible, is not.

But if the world of distinctively human culture, *relational* culture, spins 'round only on the energy of love, then perhaps it's time to dust off and replay another once-popular song and take notice of its message: "What the world needs now is love, sweet love." These lyrics were written and recorded years ago. Their message is up-to-date.

And it raises an urgent two-part question: *What is real love? And how can we move past our stubborn and subtle self-centeredness to put it on display?*

Are we suffering from a severe shortfall of real love, and is that our world's worst problem? That's one disturbing question. Here are two more: Do we even know what real love is, or has our culture, including our Christian culture, bought into a distorted counterfeit? And is it possible that after Adam and Eve had their first fight (I assume there were many more), no one except Jesus has ever purely loved anyone? A dangerous question. If the answer is yes, then what hope is there for our world?

It's true, of course, that we all can name at least one or two people who do love uncommonly well. Several older men have clearly modeled for me what it means for a husband to love his wife. A remarkable woman I know quite well radiates selfless concern for others from a heart quietly obsessed with Jesus. And yet, in some circumstances and with certain people, the lingering corruption of self-centeredness makes itself visible, however faintly, in everyone, even the most mature.

Only one person in the history of the world ever perfectly loved the way God loves, for an obvious reason: He was (and is) God! Everyone other than Jesus, from Eden till now, in some way falls short of divine love every day. We all fall short of the glory of God, the *relational* glory of the God who is love.

That's the bad news. Here's the good news, and it comes in two parts. First, not only are we fully forgiven for all sin, including our relational sin, but God's Spirit is now at work to form Jesus in us so that we can grow to love the way He loves, never completely till heaven but meaningfully now. To everyone who recognizes and hates their self-centeredness, that's good news. Second, the more Christians resemble Jesus by how we relate, the more the world of Christians will go 'round in rhythm with God's good plan. Marriages will deepen, friendships will last, and our communities will reveal to a watching world a kind of love that only Jesus makes possible.

But none of that will happen unless we recognize how we, and I'm speaking of Christians, *don't* love like Jesus. That's the first step. But pride gets in the way. We preserve a favorable self-image by lowering the divine standard of love down to a manageable level. Be nice. Serve others. As missional Christians, do good things for needy people. Sacrifice a little for the sake of others. Be faithful in your marriage. Be there for your kids. Good! We can do that, and feel pretty good about the way we love.

Do we not know? *There is a better love!* It's the love Jesus put on display. By definition, love is *relational*, not merely doing good things for others but intimately relating to others so that they feel heard, seen, valued, and accepted at their worst, with a vision for who they could become. *By Christian definition, loving is relating in a way that quite literally pours the life of God from one soul into another.* And it's costly. Real love sacrifices what we most value for the sake of another, even for someone who treats us badly. Real love suffers what we most fear if it serves the well-being of another, including someone we have reason to fear. To the degree that we glimpse real love, and in its pure form it's visible only in Jesus, our shortfall becomes evident. But it is when we glimpse the beauty of this divine love that a desire to really love comes alive in our souls. It's what we were meant to do.

We quickly realize, however, that loving like Jesus does not come easily or naturally. Of course not. He was radically other-centered. By nature, we're radically self-centered. A battle is required. A difficult path must be followed. The most important battle is not between ourselves and others. Nor is it a battle to master communication skills or to avoid defensive reactions when others offend us in hopes that our offenders will applaud our commendable efforts and treat us better. The battle for a better love is fought *in* us, in everyone whose vision of real love is coming into enough focus to expose our sometimes subtle but always ongoing love of self. It's a battle that we *want* to enter when we experience a profound yearning to put Jesus on display by how we love.

What is this battle? What exactly is the better love that is worth battling for? What happens in us if, when we battle for a better love, those we love respond poorly? Is there joy in the journey if the journey is a lifelong battle? And which brings deeper joy, receiving blessings or giving love?

Three people I've recently spoken with come to mind, people with stories that are perhaps similar to or different from yours and mine, but like you and me they need answers to these and many other related questions. Let me introduce them to you, with changed names.

The Unappreciated Pastor

For sixteen years, Mark has faithfully led his congregation as it grew from less than one hundred to now more than three hundred regular attendees. In all that time, he gladly made himself available for personal help at any hour. He felt called to *pastor*. With his wife, he had arranged dozens of social events designed to build close community, often and without complaint absorbing most of the expenses.

Mark loved to preach. He longed to bring God to his people through God's Word. Patiently, always wanting to be more effective, he had listened to criticisms of his preaching, usually presented as helpful suggestions to consider. "I think more real-life stories would make your sermons more interesting and inspiring." "The church we attended before we moved here was known for its careful expository ministry. More of that might really grow this church." "You don't talk much about social issues, like same-sex marriage and abortion. We really need to know what the Bible says about such matters."

A weary Mark told me, "It's getting really hard to love these people. I'm not even sure what that would mean. For now I mostly endure them with a pastor's smile on my face, though I did lose it last week with my worst regular critic and told him he had a bad attitude. Maybe he'll leave the church. I wouldn't miss him.

14

Am I just hopelessly insecure? I feel so unappreciated. I get one encouraging word for every two dozen criticisms. I'm not sure if I'm bitter, maybe just a bad pastor, or really tired. But I am sure that I'm not loving these people very well. Any ideas?"

The Self-Protected Wife

Sandy had been married before, for twenty years. She knew that the Bible said somewhere that God hates divorce, so she endured two long decades of nearly every kind of abuse. With the support of a new pastor who came to her church, she finally divorced her husband and, after five years as a single, remarried.

She asked me, "Do I have some kind of post-traumatic stress disorder? I've been married now for three years to a really wonderful guy. He's nothing at all like my first husband. But sometimes I explode in anger at him over the smallest things. It seems like I'm protecting myself from even the possibility of any more pain. My heart is so raw. I want to love my husband well, but I don't. I've walled myself off from him to keep myself safe, even from his genuine affection and kindness. Will I ever be free to really love him, or anyone else for that matter?"

The Yearning Disciple

I know Chuck pretty well and think he's a great guy. His wife and his adult kids think so too. So does everyone who knows him. And he loves the Bible. When he guest preaches, folks who sometimes skip church don't.

He met me for lunch yesterday, looking troubled. He got right into it. "I really do love my family and friends. And I love God and His Word. But the more I meet Jesus in the Gospels, the more I realize I don't love anyone the way He loves everyone. I don't think I'm feeling pressure to love better, I just want to. Larry, I've been in spiritual direction now for more than a year, nearly every week for an hour. And I'm experiencing God's presence more deeply. I'm grateful.

But here's what's bothering me. I'm not growing in the way I love people. I'm coming to recognize so many self-serving motives in me as I talk to my wife and kids, or anybody else. Even when I preach, I'm sometimes more aware of how I'm being received than whether the Spirit is speaking through me. I know I'll always have mixed motives. The flesh-Spirit battle will go on till I die. But I could love better. I long to love well. Is there some path I'm missing that would lead me into a better kind of love?"

Like me, each of these people is struggling to love well. You've heard their stories. What's yours? Where do you wish you could relate less impatiently, less guardedly, and more freely and genuinely, even with people you can't easily like? If you're looking for a spiritual method to get your "love act" together, this book will be no help. Again like me, you will never get it right, not until heaven. For now, celebrate God's grace not only when you succeed in loving well but also when you fail, and you'll enter the battle for a better love.

I've written this book to think through what it means to really love and to explore the truth that sets us free to relate closer to the way we wish we could, to love like Jesus. As you journey with me in the following pages, and as I share something of my path to loving more like Jesus, think about your relationships and the circumstances in which you find yourself. *What would it mean for you to battle for a better love?*

Let me suggest a few thoughts to get us started.

- The battle for a better love can only be fought on what the Lord referred to as the narrow road. We need to find that road and get on it.
- Every battle confronts an enemy. The enemy we encounter on the narrow road is our devil-inspired, world-shaped tendency

16

to arrange for our well-being at the expense of others, often by the way we relate. Relational sin, often unrecognized and usually subtle, is a vicious enemy; perhaps it's our worst.

- Those who live on the narrow road discover happiness—not always the familiar pleasant feelings that come when life goes our way but rather soul happiness, a weighty anchor that sustains us with hope and joy as we live to love.

- Our desire to experience God's presence is satisfied most fully when we express God's character most clearly by how we relate.

- Prayer is an essential weapon in the battle. The kind of prayer that pours out of us as we walk the narrow road doesn't center on the good things we legitimately want, such as good health and a decent job or even a happy family and good friends. It rather meaningfully and passionately asks God's Spirit, at any cost to ourselves, to make us little Christs who reveal the Father's heart to the world by the way we love.

What the world needs now is for the church of Jesus Christ to join together in Spirit-led community as we battle for a better love. I pray this book will help show the way.

Introduction

Nothing in today's world, including our church world, has suffered more serious distortion than our understanding of love. And for good reason. Undistorted love, sacrificially pouring yourself out for the sake of others, carries with it an unexpected and heavy cost. Jesus is the ultimate example. The cost He paid to love us, in Gethsemane and on Calvary, was heavy enough to surprise even Him.

And nothing in modern culture has been more weakly defined than happiness, that rare inner awareness of a quietly contented sense of well-being that we cannot help but long to experience. And that fact, that we cannot extinguish our desire to be happy, suggests that perhaps we were created by a happy God to be happy—to be happy *like* God.

But most of us settle for less. We prefer to enjoy the good feelings that rise up within us when we are noticed, wanted, and respected by others; when things go well in our lives, according to our plans; and when we do fun things. We then often demand whatever produces the good feelings we want and feel bad when our demands go unmet.

Let's call those good feelings "second thing happiness." That kind of happiness is good and rightly enjoyed, when available. I like feeling loved by my family and friends. I feel good when my doctor tells me the surgery went well. I enjoy playing golf, more so when my drive finds the fairway. But my desire for second thing happiness leaves me dependent on things beyond my control in order to feel good.

"First thing happiness" is entirely different. It feels different and its source is different. First thing happiness, in God's thinking a better kind of happiness, develops when we struggle to love others with a costly love that is possible only if we have a life-giving relationship with Jesus that is grounded entirely in His love for us. This love lets us rest, not complacently but comfortably, in our ongoing weakness and failure.

But there's a problem—actually many. Here's one. The notion that the happiness we most long to know comes from loving others sacrificially, the way Jesus loved us when He was crucified, is too easily heard as a worthy ideal that is more romantic than realistic. Loving others with their well-being in view at any cost to us is a lovely thought, but when others treat us poorly or when life gets too rough that kind of love seems unworkable, too difficult, and really quite foolish. It's time then to protect ourselves, to look out for our own immediately felt well-being. If we're to be happy, or at least safe, self-protection makes more sense than self-sacrifice. So we think.

Anita came to a conference I led on learning to love like Jesus and left deeply stirred. "I can see now that I've felt entitled to hold a grudge against my husband for treating me like I barely exist," she said. "His neglect really hurts me, but I want to put Jesus on display by the way I treat him. I'm so excited to get home."

A month later, I received this email from her:

> Larry, I tried. But it didn't work. My husband hasn't changed one bit. He seems even more irritable toward me. And the happiness you talked about at the conference never came. If I don't back away to protect myself from him I think I'd die. I'm sorry, but I just can't love this man. He hurts me too much.

My follow-up phone conversation with Anita made two things clear. First, she was assuming that Jesus-like love meant no confrontation, not letting her husband know the impact he was having on her. Second, she expected to feel a kind of happiness that would eliminate whatever hurt she felt from her husband's angry indifference. If she loved him, she assumed either he would begin treating her well or God would miraculously provide a joy that would drown her sorrow. She had a difficult time appreciating that the happiness the Spirit provides when we love like Jesus exists *beneath* the hurt another causes us. It is a happiness experienced as a solid sense of "mission accomplished," of delighting God by revealing to others the love He displayed to the world through His Son.

Nothing in today's world, including our church world, has been more lamentably treated as fiction, if it is even considered, than the God-arranged connection between loving others and finding happiness. If Jesus is our model, then loving others sacrificially generates a kind of happiness, an awareness of destiny fulfilled, that remains alive even when life is unjustly difficult and our hearts feel empty and alone. Jesus, the Man of Sorrows. Was He happy? Yes, with a kind of happiness most of us are unaware we want. More on that later.

Loving like Jesus, self-sacrificially and not self-protectively, produces first thing happiness. If we think we're loving others and don't experience something identifiable as joy, it would be good to wonder if we're really loving anybody.

What exactly do sincerely caring parents mean when they tell their children "we just want you to be happy"? Are they perhaps wanting to feel good because their children feel good? What then happens to their happiness if their children fail or rebel, or become depressed or angry? How are Christian spouses thinking about love and happiness when they say to themselves, *I am so unhappy in my marriage. I know Jesus wants me to love my spouse. But I don't. I can't. I'm hurting too much.* Is happiness available to a spouse in a marriage that doesn't get better?

How does a distorted view of love and a weak understanding of happiness encourage us to respond when a close friend betrays us or in some other way hurts us deeply? Is our happiness dependent on that friend repenting? Second thing happiness is. But is there a way to love our unloving friend that releases in us a happiness not dependent on the response we understandably desire from another?

One more scenario. Does Jesus actually intend that we love a parent who for years has been nothing but annoying, sometimes abusive? Did He really command us to love a parent we would just as soon never see again, a parent who never meaningfully parented us? Is that possible, or even good? If we graciously smiled and simply put up with the hurt we feel, would it not just enable the self-addicted parent the same way we would enable an alcoholic by kindly pouring him another drink?

Or is there a new way to love that parent, a way that would provide God's Spirit access into that mother's or father's heart and at the same time leave us happy whether our parent received the Spirit's work or not? If our view of love is distorted and our understanding of happiness is weak, what we might imagine it would mean to love that parent would be impossible—or at least unreasonable and foolish. And our hope for happiness in that relationship would lie in our parent learning to love us well.

Three Groups

The questions I am raising come down to these:

- Is there a kind of love, a better kind, that brings joy when it is given, not when it meets with a satisfying response from another?
- Is there a kind of happiness that survives both the most damaging relational pain caused by another and the most discouraging and devastating of circumstances?
- Is there a connection, a cause-effect relationship, between offering undistorted love and experiencing strong happiness?

- Is Jesus-like happiness experienced as a good feeling, or is it better known as a living and sustaining reality, an awareness of both loving life as it should be lived and a freedom to do so?

As I prepare to engage these questions in this book, three groups of people come to mind.

Group 1

This group contains those who, in response to disappointing relationships or difficult circumstances, live most days with low or high levels of misery. These folks experience neither first nor second thing happiness. They are simply unhappy most of the time and often just miserable.

You likely belong in this group if the way you are being treated by someone who matters to you leaves you feeling angrily and protectively defensive, in your own eyes deservedly determined to be treated fairly, and by your own reckoning justifiably diminished in your enthusiasm to be there for anyone more than for yourself. Perhaps shattered dreams have left you grumpily or nobly resigned to living as a self-pitying victim in an unjust world.

To you I say: *walk the narrow road to life*. If you know Jesus and therefore possess a nature made of the same stuff as God's nature, you can discover a kind of happiness that can be yours even if nothing outside of you changes. But you must learn what it means to walk the narrow road that Jesus said leads to life. Only then will you enjoy the fruit of loving well.

Group 2

These people have lives that are going well enough to supply them with a regular dose of second thing happiness. You might belong in this group if you experience yourself as generally happy, as someone who most often feels pretty good. You don't need to know Jesus to belong to this group, though many assume that they know Jesus *because* they belong to this group, because they enjoy life and feel good.

Your membership in group 2 is confirmed if, when asked why you are happy, your mind naturally goes to the blessings you enjoy, perhaps a chipper disposition or a fulfilling ministry or a satisfying marriage or an important job or financial stability or good health or close friends.

To you I say: *I'm glad for you.* Blessings are good. They are God's provision. Second thing happiness is meant to be enjoyed. But the happiness of blessings is both fickle and dangerous. It is a tenuous happiness that continues only if relationships and circumstances continue to go well. And blessings, though rightly appreciated, are dangerous, as is the happiness they provide. A blessed life might encourage you to settle for enjoying less than what God has made available to you. A pleasant life requires only pleasant love to enjoy.

A difficult life requires costly love, a better one that brings peace in the middle of storms. Suffering has unique power to put you in touch with undistorted love, the kind that has opportunity to come more alive when relationships sour and circumstances unravel. Too often, a blessed life leaves distorted love unrecognized and unchallenged.

Consider a new way to understand both love and happiness, a way that will move you onto the narrow road where you will no longer depend on life's blessings for your happiness, though you will still gratefully enjoy them. Instead you will discover undistorted love, a way to love that lets you know the happiness of Jesus.

Group 3

This group of people live with a consuming thirst for living water. These folks know that living water bubbles up within them when it pours out of them into others. From experience they know the refreshing water that flows into them from others will reach deep into their hearts but ultimately fail to quench their deepest thirst, and therefore will leave them more thirsty for satisfaction that seems less available.

You belong in this group if you long to enjoy who God is and who He is to you more than you enjoy anyone or anything else. Your identity in group 3 is confirmed if you celebrate who God is by wanting to reveal Him to others and by pouring His love into others, even though doing so sometimes deepens an already deep emptiness within you, an emptiness that intensifies your thirst for God.

In your embraced emptiness and welcomed thirst, you experience a greater freedom to love with no expectation that your emptiness or thirst will be fully relieved but rather with the expectation that in your unrelieved emptiness and thirst there is a way to be happy. You come to realize that it is your *thirst* for God that sustains you in your commitment to love others more than your *experience* of God. You enjoy God's presence now only in measure. Only in heaven, when you see Christ face-to-face, will you experience His beauty with unmeasured delight. The greater your enjoyment of Him in this life, the more passionately you thirst *now* to experience more of His beauty until *then*, when your deepest thirst will be forever quenched. Sustaining thirst for God is a sure mark of a group 3 Christian.

To you I say: *thank God for His work in your life.* Distorted love, the kind that not only excuses but justifies self-protective relating, is giving way to undistorted love, to the costly love of self-sacrifice that reveals God's nature and the way He relates. The cost is real, but the cost is worth it. You are coming to know the power of kingdom living, of loving in a way that brings God's relational kingdom into your sphere of influence.

You may at times experience a worrisome distance from those you love. But that felt distance may not be evidence that your love is weak; rather it likely reveals that your love is strong enough to require no satisfying response from others in order for your love to continue pouring into them. What passes for intimacy in our culture, both secular and religious, is too often little more than receiving from another what we demand. True intimacy develops when true love is offered, the kind that desires but doesn't demand a response.

For no apparent reason, your feeling of love and your desire to love will sometimes fade. It is then that your will to love will become singularly necessary. It was will that kept Jesus on the cross. Exercise that will, and slowly but reliably you will know the happiness that Jesus knew, in small but sustaining measure. You will then gratefully and with delight realize that you are on the narrow road to life.

Distorted love delivers a fragile and narcissistic happiness. Correcting this distortion is resisted for good reason: undistorted love, a love that sacrifices one's self for the well-being of others, allows no illegitimate self-protection and thus makes us vulnerable to pain we could avoid.

Undistorted love is worth fighting for. It is divine love, the love of God revealed in both His three-Person community and in His gospel, a love that when alive in us embraces self-sacrifice as a privileged opportunity. We learn to surrender lesser pleasures, the demand to experience second thing happiness, in order to make room for the first thing happiness that emerges when we love like Jesus, when we relate to others in a way that delights God and enlivens our souls. Intimacy with God, the enjoyment of His presence, develops to a significant degree as we learn to love like God.

This book is about the battle for a better love, the struggle to love others with undistorted love that brings with it both suffering and happiness. It is a battle that will not be fully won until heaven. And the battle will only be productively engaged in this world if we walk the narrow road to life. But we must be clear. *It is a battle.* And I invite you to join me in the discussion of what it means to find that road and walk on it as we battle to love.

One More Introductory Note:
Are Happiness and Joy Different?

I will be using the words *happiness* and *joy* interchangeably through-out this book. Is that legitimate or not? Do those words refer to one experience or two? The question needs an answer. Let me provide one: yes . . . and no! It depends on how you define the terms.

If the question interests you, read on. If not, skip to the next chapter.

In most Christian circles, the answer is an immediate yes: the two are different. Happiness, it is commonly assumed, has a different source than joy, and the *feeling* of happiness is not at all the same as the *experience* of joy. Most of us understand happiness to be the always pleasant, sometimes elated, occasionally giddy emotion we feel when our lives are going well, when good news comes our way.

Joy, we think, is different. It is not a pleasurable feeling gener-ated by desirable circumstances. Joy is more than an itch finally scratched, more than a request granted or a wish fulfilled. In its deepest and most spiritual form, joy is thought to be the anchor-ing reality of being able, with conviction, to say *it is well with my soul* not because life is unfolding in a way that is to our liking but because we trust the God whose loving presence we meaningfully experience.

Given that understanding, the answer to the question is an un-arguable yes: happiness and joy are different. But something I've observed gives me pause with this answer: neither seemingly happy nor joyful Christians reliably love well.

Some do, of course, but many don't, not like Jesus. It seems to me that a predictable relationship should exist between both hap-piness and joy and the ability to love well. Think about it. If joy is delighting in the felt presence of a loving God, then the experience of joy should reveal itself in the way we love others. Sometimes it does. Some Christians who report that they experience real joy in being loved by God gladly pour that same love into others. Some don't.

And happy Christians, freed from worry by the enjoyment of blessings, might be expected to concern themselves with the well-being of others. Sometimes they do. But neither happy Christians who enjoy their lives nor joyful Christians who enjoy God's presence reliably love others, at least not with the costly love of Jesus.

The Christians I know who love in ways that make me yearn to love with a better love—their number is few and one in particular comes to mind—deeply feel the unhappiness that accompanies shattered dreams and, regrettably too often, sense God's absence when they most long to feel His presence. They understand what John of the Cross meant when he spoke of dark nights of the soul. As we commonly define happiness and joy, these few Christians frequently experience neither. *And yet they evidence a stronger commitment to the well-being of others than to their own.*

The man who comes to my mind illustrates this point. Soon after a terrible tragedy in his family, I spoke with him. He shared the depths of his unhappiness and his longing to know God in ways he had not yet experienced. But quickly, without denying his thirsty anguish, he poured his energy into knowing how I was doing. Happy Christians seem more inclined to revel in their happiness than to explore the world of another. Similarly, joyful Christians sometimes talk more of their experiences of God than, with loving curiosity, wonder about the spiritual journey of others.

Ask my loving but unhappy and joyless friend (unhappy and joyless according to our usual definitions) if he knows the happiness of Jesus, and he quietly answers, "Yes." Ask him if he knows the Spirit's fruit of joy, and with restful certainty he replies, "Of course." *What does he mean?*

Is it possible to know the happiness of Jesus by loving like Jesus even when we experience little, perhaps nothing, of His presence? Can we feel contentedly settled with the awareness of realized destiny, of fulfilling our life's purpose as Christians called to bring the light of divine love into the dark places of another's soul, even when the darkness of loneliness and sorrow overwhelms ours?

From personal experience, I understand why unhappy Christians plagued by difficult circumstances and painful relationships have little interest in someone else's problems when theirs feel so consuming. And again from personal experience, I appreciate how unnatural it is to be there for others when the sense of God's absence generates the darkness of despair. And yet as Jesus hung on the cross, He did exactly that! With neither the happiness of pleasant circumstances nor the joy of experiencing His Father's gentle presence, Jesus chose to endure torture of body and soul that one nod toward heaven would have immediately ended. Why? Why not a pain-ending nod? Because *He was committed to my well-being at any cost to Himself, all to reveal the glory of His Father's unfathomable love.* "We know what real love is because Jesus gave up his life for us" (1 John 3:16).

Can I ever love like Jesus? What will it take? Was it redefined happiness and joy that empowered Him to love so sacrificially? Was Jesus happy not only when He provided wine at a wedding but also while nails were pounded into His hands and feet? Was He joyful not only after His resurrection but also during His crucifixion? In our natural way of understanding happiness and joy, the answer is an obvious and loud no. He endured the cross. In no sense did Jesus enjoy either the torture of crucifixion or the devastating absence of His Father. But there is a way to understand happiness and joy that has been long forgotten and is radically unique.

A truth I will explore throughout the pages of this book is both simple and profound: *Jesus's happiness and joy came from giving Himself.* Is giving ourselves really the path to the joy we most want? Would I long to truly love if I understood that truth, and if I then longed to know His happiness and joy?

I'm told the early Greek philosophers defined happiness as living congruently with one's deepest nature. Would that define joy as well?

Certainly that is exactly how Jesus lived. In Him we get an up-front view of God's essential nature of *outwardness*, the glad passion to share with others the pleasure He knows, the pleasure only Jesus can provide. Jonathan Edwards once wrote that the entire purpose of the gospel is to communicate the happiness of Jesus to His followers, to deliver His nature of outwardness into the center of our being, and to then guide us onto the narrow road of relating congruently with that divine passion, no longer always curved in on ourselves but increasingly often poured out for others.

Is it possible, then, to know God, to experience the beauty of divine love, and to *not* reveal some significant measure of Christ's suffering, self-denying outwardness by how we relate?

Listen to the apostle John's answer. "Anyone who claims to live in God's light and hates a brother or sister is still in the dark" (2:9 MSG). In John's mind, the absence of love suggests the presence of hate. And our answer must be no. If we experience God's love, it is impossible not to, in some measure, express God's love to another. To do so may involve a battle, but it's a battle the beloved of God will enter.

Inwardness, a priority commitment to my own felt well-being that only when honored frees me to care about you, too often passes for love. It is not. Inwardness falls woefully short of the relational beauty of God's outwardness. Outwardness is love, self-denial for the sake of another. Inwardness is hate, self-love that eclipses love for others.

If a follower of Jesus claims to know God, to experience the presence of Jesus, but relates more inwardly than outwardly, that person's claim is suspect. Their experience of joy is counterfeit. Their feeling of happiness is no different than the happiness of a non-Christian whose life is going well.

The question now comes to a head: What is joy, and is it different than happiness? Some redefinition seems necessary. Joy, the fruit only of God's Spirit, depends for its existence neither on pleasurable circumstances nor on rich experiences of God's presence. *The joy of fellowship with the Trinity develops when we relate like the Trinity as Jesus is formed in us by His Spirit.*

And happiness that exists only when life treats us well, though properly welcomed, is second thing happiness. It is not the deep happiness of Jesus that we can know in this life. Consider the sources of second thing happiness.

- *Life goes well.* Blessings overflow. We feel happy.
- *We do well.* We achieve a long-desired goal. We feel happy.
- *We experience God's presence.* Perhaps through worship music, time in the Bible, or the practice of spiritual disciplines, we sense that God is with us. We feel happy. We may call it joy.

But if the emotions aroused by any of the above sources do not lead us into the battle for a better love, the love revealed in the crucified Jesus, we have not yet tasted the deep happiness and the true joy of Jesus. We are experiencing only second thing happiness. It is right to enjoy the feeling. It is wrong to call it joy.

Not only a different kind of joy but also a different kind of happiness, first thing happiness, is available to those who follow Jesus onto the narrow road. It animates the soul of a Christian who, living loved, *therefore lives to love.* It is the fruit of God's Spirit. It is joy. It is happiness of the first thing variety. Defined this way, the two are one. The *experience* of God's love that results in the *expression* of God's love brings joy, first thing happiness. Jesus lived what He taught: "You're far happier giving than getting" (Acts 20:35 MSG).

Perhaps now that question can be answered: Are happiness and joy different?

Second thing happiness or felt pleasure that comes with the blessings of life, including the wonderful blessing of being treated well by others, the achievement of goals, or the felt experience of God's presence, is legitimate and legitimately enjoyed. But it is not joy. *Yes, second thing happiness and joy are different.*

First thing happiness, realized purpose that comes with knowing the better love of Jesus in a way that inflames a burning desire and an enlivening thirst to pour that better love into others, is experienced as the anchoring reality of joy when that desire is indulged, when we love like Jesus. The experience of God becomes true joy when we express God's outward nature by how we relate. *No, first thing happiness and joy are not different.* They are the same, one Spirit-granted reality.

Christians are thirsty both to know God and to reveal God. The pursuit of knowing God as He is in His eternal community and of knowing what He is doing in this disappointing and difficult world generates an insatiable thirst to make known to others who He is and what He is up to.

All that to say this: in this book, when I speak of the happiness available to Jesus followers who walk the narrow road to relational life, unless I specify that I'm referring to second thing happiness that sometimes accompanies travelers on the narrow road, know that I am speaking of the first thing happiness released in us when we battle for a better love. That kind of happiness is unmistakably the Spirit's doing. It is joy.

Three Passages to Ponder As You Now Explore the Message of This Book

Enter by the narrow gate. For the gate is wide and the way is easy that leads to destruction, and those who enter by it are many. For the gate is narrow and the way is hard that leads to life, and those who find it are few.

Jesus

Don't tell us what is right. Tell us nice things. Tell us lies. Forget all this gloom. Get off your narrow path. Stop telling us about your "Holy One of Israel."

The Many

The LORD says, "I will guide you along the best pathway for your life." . . . I hear the tumult of the raging seas as your waves and surging tides sweep over me. But each day the LORD pours his unfailing love upon me, and through each night I sing his songs, praying to God who gives me life.

The Few[1]

PART 1

THE GOOD NEWS
THAT SOUNDS BAD

Follow Me.

Where will You take me?

To real life.

How will I get there?

I will lead you on a rough road.

Isn't there an easier way?

1

Does Anyone Want to Be Happy, Like Jesus?

Not too many years ago, in the church my younger son's family then attended, I was meeting with the elders, church staff, and worship team before the Sunday service. I was the guest preacher. After the order of service was outlined and before we prayed, the pastor, a good friend who knew me well, introduced me to the group.

"Most of you are familiar with Dr. Crabb. I know many of you have read a few of his books. One of our Sunday school classes is right now studying his popular but challenging *Shattered Dreams*. He told me earlier this morning that the title he's given to his sermon today is 'Happiness in the Christian Life.'"

He then paused. With a straight face and with no attempt at either sarcasm or humor, he added, "You probably realize that Dr. Crabb is not known for that topic, so I'm sure we'll all be eager to hear his thoughts on what it means to be happy. It might be good if we spent some time in prayer now, for Dr. Crabb and for what we're about to hear."

If you are at all familiar with my earlier work, you know that for forty years I've been exploring the dark side of life, our troubled existence in this mixed-up world. I've thought hard about our love of sin and the heartaches that result, as well as tragedies that have no apparent explanation. And I've treated life's struggles as opportunities to know God better, to be spiritually formed no matter what may be happening in us or to us or around us. I've wanted to understand how a good God uses all that is bad in our lives to make us holy.

I'm not known, and I've never wanted to be, for encouraging people to be happy *as most of us commonly understand happiness.* I'm glad for the happiness people, including me, experience while vacationing at Disney World or at a beachfront resort, or when family, friendships, health, and finances are all doing well. But that kind of happiness—second thing happiness—can erode the desire to pay whatever price is required to know God so well that we discover first thing happiness, the true joy that develops only as we love like Jesus.

Let me be as clear as I can be about one thing: loving like Jesus means loving people while they sin and not loving them more when they celebrate victory over some specific sin. But let me be clear about one more thing: even the most spiritual among us will never love exactly like Jesus in this life.

And when we fail badly to love well, God does not love us less. He is then glorified as the God whose grace is so amazing that it is always provided, whether we love well or not. But the more we celebrate His grace that loves us at our worst, the more we will long to battle for the better love we receive from Jesus.

It follows that our richest happiness depends not on loving like Jesus but on knowing we are loved with extravagant grace by Jesus. And the more we rest in His inexplicable love, the more God's Spirit, in His time, will release us to show that grace to others and the more happiness we will experience.

My fond hope—and I think it is realistic—is that one day someone will suggest the following epitaph to be engraved on my tombstone:

Here lies a man who all his life was preoccupied with what it means to be happy like Jesus.

From my early days of ministry as a young psychologist, I've believed that because God is love God is happy, and I've thought for a long time that a relationship exists between loving others and being happy. I've confidently assumed that somehow God is happy, supremely happy, with a happiness He wants me to enjoy, a happiness He enjoys in spite of the suffering that His love for people like me inevitably brings.

More recently, I've come to see something that surprised me: the happy God of suffering love is happy *while He suffers.* Even more remarkably and with sober excitement, I've been persuaded that, at least in part, He experiences a certain kind of happiness *because He suffers.* Certainly He was happy in eternity past when in His divine community there was no suffering. But a deep happiness always alive within each member of the Trinity was revealed when God created people to love who then turned away from Him. It is in His experience of suffering that His unique passion of love is most fully revealed.

It is making fresh sense to me to understand, only a little and from a great distance, that it is the willingness to suffer for the happiness of another, even for others who are foolishly seeking their happiness elsewhere, that reveals the extraordinary nature and unfathomable depths of divine love.

In the gospel, Jesus came to tell us the good news that God wants every follower of Jesus to be happy with the happiness of Jesus, and that He is willing to pay any price required to make that happiness available. Not only did Jesus die to make it available but He lived to reveal what it looks like for a human being to know the happiness that comes from relating to others with divine love, even when living in a world stained by human misery brought on by human self-centeredness.

It is vitally important that we gain a clear understanding, albeit limited, of the happiness of Jesus that is now available to us and how we must love in order to enjoy it.

Ever since Jesus came into this world as a human being, lived in a way that put divine love on display in human relating, died to reveal the depths of that love, was resurrected so that He could pour divine love into our human hearts, and then returned to heaven to make room for His Spirit to come into us in a new way, something breathtaking has been going on. It's happening right this moment.

Right now the Spirit of Jesus, the Spirit of the love that makes the Father and Son one in delight and purpose, is making available to every Christian the happiness Jesus knew:

- *when* He danced with the wedding guests at Cana as they were enjoying the fine wine He supplied. We're not told Jesus danced, but if the wedding guests were dancing, I assume He joined in. Picture Jesus dancing, holding a glass of wine. It's a good image.
- *when* He wept at the tomb of Lazarus, feeling angry that death was now part of life. Then, I imagine with a big smile, Jesus welcomed Lazarus as he walked out of his grave when Jesus told him to.
- *when*, feeling deeply disappointed, Jesus spoke firmly but gently to the three disciples who had fallen asleep after He had asked them to share His sorrow over His impending crucifixion.
- *when*, soon after, He looked at Peter with eyes filled with forgiveness, compassion, and hope, into the eyes of the brash, self-confessed loyal follower of Jesus who had just betrayed Him three times.
- *when*, even when, He was mercilessly whipped and then nailed to a cross to die a slow, horrific death.
- *when* He shouted "It is finished!" then told His Father He was coming home.

- *when* He amazed His grieving disciples by greeting them on the first Easter morning, having died on Friday and now revealed to be alive on Sunday.
- *when* He promised to always be with His disciples as they paid a stiff price to make more disciples of Jesus.
- *when*, now seated at the Father's right hand, He continues to tell His story of suffering love through you and me as we share in His happiness by loving as He did.

Pause for a moment. Could that be true? Was Jesus truly *happy* in each of those circumstances? If so, and I believe He was, then why? And what kind of happiness did He experience? It seems preposterously unthinkable to claim that Jesus was in any sense happy as He hung on the cross, especially during those dreadful three hours of darkness when all felt awareness of His Father's loving presence had vanished. Whatever kind of happiness He knew in those moments is not the kind of happiness I naturally want. The happiness of relieved pain and enjoyed blessings has more appeal.

But consider this. If Jesus was always filled with and ruled by the Holy Spirit's passion of undistorted love, the kind that finds joy in suffering for others, and if the fruit of the Spirit includes joy, then we must conclude the unthinkable: always, in His pleasant moments at the Cana wedding and in His suffering moments on Calvary, *Jesus knew the happiness that accompanies suffering love.* (See appendix for a discussion of the question: Was Jesus filled with God's Spirit when His Father abandoned Him on the cross?)

We must be clear. Jesus endured no suffering as a helpless, unwilling victim. He was always willing and therefore not primarily a victim at all but rather a free agent choosing to suffer on behalf of people who were unworthy of His love. It is that kind of love, undistorted by self-centeredness, that brings the happiness we were created to enjoy even in the darkest night.

41

This is radical stuff. To be happy with the happiness of Jesus, then, means to know happiness can coexist with the worst anguish a human can experience. But this happiness comes only if we express the sacrificial love of Jesus at the same time as we endure anguish. Let me state the obvious: we need to profoundly redefine both what it means to be happy with the happiness that was always alive in Jesus and what it means to love others with undistorted love, the way Jesus loved. We need to get in touch with our deep desire to love like Jesus and to be happy like Jesus.

I see this book as the next installment in the story I've been longing to tell for nearly half a century. The story is a good one. Perhaps I've told it poorly but I know this story lets us hear good news straight from heaven—the good news, for followers of Jesus as they live in this world, that in any circumstance of life, no matter how difficult or terrifying, and in any condition of soul, no matter how empty or alone, disciples of Jesus can know His happiness. This happiness arises from Jesus's love and sustains us in putting His love on display by how we relate to others. The happiness of Jesus can be ours if we fight the battle to love, a battle that can be won, never fully till heaven but substantially now, only on the narrow road.

Perhaps one day I'll be known as a happy disciple of Jesus, someone who learned a little of what it means to love like Jesus. I'll then surprise no one when I announce that I'll be preaching on happiness in the Christian life. I want to experience that reality, and if it advances God's purposes, to be known as someone who does.

2

Good News in Any Difficult
Relationship or Circumstance

If the life to which the narrow road leads refers to spiritual maturity, then the process of learning to love like Jesus includes difficulty. To hear that the road that leads us to our desired destination is narrow does not provide much hope that traveling on that road through life in this world will be easy.

Mark, the unappreciated pastor, illustrates the point. After wearily acknowledging that he felt more irritable than gracious toward most folks in his congregation, he asked if I had any ideas that might free him to love them better.

Knowing that tips on how to love don't change the heart, where the real problem lies, I asked Mark, "Why do you want to love them well?"

"Well, that's a question I didn't expect. Christians, maybe especially pastors, are supposed to love everyone."

I was concerned that, like many of us, Mark thought of loving merely as doing good for people rather than relating well with them. So I asked, "Loving the way you're supposed to love means what?"

"Isn't it obvious? Forgiving people, being kind to them; you know, things like that. But that's what I'm having a hard time doing. Sometimes I just want to quit being a pastor."

"If there's not a way to desire to love them, you never will."

"I agree. So is there a way?"

"Yes, but it might not appeal to you."

Spiritually maturing followers of Jesus are not recognizable merely by their faithful church attendance, gifted Bible teaching, large following, generous giving, championing of Christian principles in government and society, or even by a lifestyle of moral choices and good deeds. Lukewarm Christians can be known for all these good things. But only wholehearted followers of Jesus who see how He sacrifices for those He loves are capable of *wanting* to love like Jesus.

No disciple, no matter how surrendered, loves perfectly. Everyone fails. But spiritually maturing disciples are passionately, hopefully, and patiently obsessed with learning to love like Jesus; they want to reveal even to hurtful family members and frustrating friends the heart of Jesus by the way they relate to others. No matter how difficult or discouraging life becomes, they long to worship God with a genuine freedom that puts them in touch with the Spirit-granted desire and ability to love everyone they encounter with Jesus-like love.

As a by-product of learning a little of what it means to love like Jesus, these disciples become aware of something deeply centered and solid within them: the happiness of Jesus. That something, a strange kind of happiness that lives beneath the deepest sorrow and survives the worst suffering, develops only as they walk the narrow road to life, a challenge few welcome.

When Jesus told His prospective followers that the road to life was narrow, their first impulse—similar to mine now—was to back away. "Jesus," I can imagine them saying, "we thought You came to bring good news. Are You really telling us that following You means trouble? In this life, are we to expect and for some reason look forward to problems and heartaches? If we're hearing You right, You're letting us know that on this narrow road to enjoying whatever it is You're calling life, we're going to feel so squeezed by its narrowness that sometimes we'll barely be able to breathe. Nothing about that seems appealing.

"Forgive us, Jesus, but what makes all this grief worth it? If a broad road would make for an easier trip through life, why wouldn't we choose it? What exactly is this life to which the narrow road is leading? And why must the way to the good You want us to experience take us through so much that feels bad? Are the difficulties necessary? Is this really *good* news?"

The word *gospel* means good news. Without question, Jesus thinks what He is telling us is good news. But it may not be the sort of news we can easily hear as good. When Christians hear the phrase "the good news of the gospel of Jesus Christ," our minds readily move toward familiar teaching that we're quite willing to agree is good news: Jesus died to pay the penalty for our sins. When we accept Him as our Savior, we're immediately forgiven for everything we've done wrong or ever will do that's wrong; we're accepted into His family and guaranteed an eternal spot in heaven. That is good news, and there's none better for those who realize where unforgiven sin would take us, in this life and especially in the next.

But too often we say "Thank You, Jesus," then turn our attention to the good news we want to hear next, good news about what will happen in our lives before we get to heaven. Here's where, usually without giving it much thought, we become naively presumptuous. We have our own comfortable ideas of what that good news should be.

Will the biopsy come back negative? That would be good news. God has the power to see to it. I won't get Alzheimer's, will I? That would be bad news. I'll pray against the devil in order to keep my mind from losing its sharp edge. And I'm counting on God to work through me so that our kids turn out well. I'm doing my part as a parent. I assume God will do His. Won't He? Shouldn't He, as reward for my obedient efforts to train my children in His ways? And won't people eventually appreciate me if I do good and treat them well? That would be good news I'd love to hear.

Can you hear the focus on self in all that thinking, the absence of worship?

It seems that our ears have become so clogged with earthbound talk about the good life God wants us to enjoy, a life of abundant blessings and healing, that we have trouble hearing the news Jesus really brings to us as supremely good, the news that we can actually learn to love like Him. That's a spiritual blessing, coming down to us from heavenly places.

We need to be clear: the gospel of Jesus is good news that is grounded in three phases. It *begins* with our forgiveness; we literally become sons and daughters in God's family. It *ends* when we forever live with God in a community and a city that is good far beyond our ability to imagine. And it centers *now* in our being spiritually formed in the middle of a seemingly random assortment of blessings, trials, healing, and pain—formed to love well, more like Jesus loves.

We also need to be clear on something else that is easily missed: *spiritual formation is relational formation.* It is easier, and therefore more talked about, to practice spiritual disciplines in an effort to feel God's presence than to practice them in order to draw on the Spirit's power to love well. Spiritually forming people may or may not regularly *experience* God with them. But spiritually forming people will grow to increasingly *reveal* God's nature by how they relate.

The point is important. The agony of hell—and its foretaste now—is the suffering of being unable to love. Imagine: people trapped in pure selfishness, living the death of isolation, always demanding what they desperately want but no one gives; image-bearers no longer capable of reflecting the nature of the One whose image they still bear. That's hell. We can taste it now.

For everyone in Christ, the vision is quite the opposite. The joy of heaven will find its never-ending source in always and fully experiencing the presence of the Father, the love of Jesus, and the life of the Spirit. The overflow will be our uncompromised ability to love others with perfect love, eternally freed to relate from pure selflessness, forever wanting only to live the joy of living loved and loving in a world made new where everyone loves like Jesus. That's a party, and we're invited.

That's the good news coming then—later, not now. But what is the good news for today, for as long as we live in this imperfect world as imperfect people? The answer is clear, and it is indeed good. But only those in touch with their deepest desire as redeemed image-bearers will hear what Jesus makes possible for us to experience now as good news. As long as the good news Mark most wants to hear is that his congregation appreciates him, he will not discover the deepest desire in his Spirit-invaded soul, the desire to love flawed people the way Jesus loves him.

The biopsy may come back malignant. We or a loved one may develop Alzheimer's. Our marriage may never live up to our expectations and hopes. Our children may break our hearts. Christian leaders may receive increasingly hurtful criticism. What, then, is the guaranteed good news of the gospel for right now, for me and for you as we live together in this world?

It is this: the Spirit of God is freeing us from our defensive, self-protective, and proud self-enhancing ways of relating and is forming us to love like Jesus. This, at the very least, means to live committed to the well-being of others at any cost to ourselves:

- in any circumstance of life, no matter how dream-shattering.
- in any relationship, no matter how disappointing or hurtful.
- in any condition of soul, no matter how dark or terrifying.

That's how Jesus loved. And, by God's grace and with the Spirit's provision of power, we're called and equipped to put Him on display by how we relate to others. But we must know this: the process of being relationally formed to love like Jesus will only go forward on the narrow road. Loving well is not easy. The road that carries us there is marked by relational land mines that blow up without warning, leaving us maimed from anger, jealousy, greed, guilt, frustration, and indifference, seemingly unable and at least for a season unwilling to love, or having no idea what it would mean to love a particularly difficult person.

But why? Questions rise up in my mind.

- What exactly is the narrow road?
- What is the relationally forming process that only happens as we travel on the narrow road through life?
- What does it actually mean to live my life on that road?
- And why must the process of being released to love more and more like Jesus unfold only on a road that can feel like it's squeezing the life out of us? (Should I say it's squeezing the hell out of us? That might be more theologically accurate.)

I begin this book with two core convictions. One: in this life, there is no real and sustaining joy other than learning to love like Jesus. That is the life to which the narrow road leads. Two: only a few even find the road that leads to life, and fewer remain on it while the forming process unfolds.

I want to be one of the few. If you want to be one of the few as well, join me as together we ask God to reveal to us what it means to live on the narrow road to life.

There is good news to hear, in any relationship or circumstance, no matter how difficult. Joy awaits as we follow Jesus on the narrow road. We can be happy with the happiness of Jesus. God thinks that is good news indeed. We can learn to think so as well.

3

Am I on the
Narrow Road to Life?

The few people who know me well, who see beneath the persona I sometimes project to the person I really am, would, I think easily and perhaps with a chuckle, agree that I would make a sorry poster boy for what many today believe a mature Christian should look like. And I think they're right.

Didn't Jesus come to give His followers "a rich and satisfying life" (John 10:10)? And wouldn't that mean a continually diminishing struggle with sin, perhaps a few small blunders along the way but certainly no need for daily repentance? And how could anyone claim to be leading a rich and satisfying life if they didn't feel pretty good about themselves and their lives and if they weren't enjoying God's blessings as a token of His favor on their sincere love for Jesus?

If that is what it means to be mature, then it's true: I am a poor advertisement for the abundant life that Jesus makes available to His followers. My critics are vocal. Several books have been written to expose how I have allegedly smuggled secular psychology into my theology, qualifying me as a psycho-heretic. I believe I have been badly misunderstood. My response? Publicly, quite gracious. But much goes on in my private world that if expressed fully would spread little of the fragrance of Jesus.

Few days pass without my feeling, at least in moments, insecure, angry, drained, weary in well-doing, defeated and discouraged, bored, worried about tomorrow, angry about today, and irritated with someone. It's true that most often few folks would realize that such weak ugliness is simmering within me. I do quite well at not allowing how I feel to determine how I behave. But beneath the surface rancid sewage continues to splash about in my depths.

It's also true that few days pass without honesty requiring me to plead guilty to relational sin, the subtle kind of sin that we think deserves only glide-by attention. We commit this sin every time we relate to someone with something less than the pure, other-centered, and perfectly God-revealing love of Jesus. I have never, not even for a moment, loved anyone with the perfectly pure love that defines the character of God. Every day I fall short of the relational glory of divine love. At least a taint, and sometimes a torrent, of self-centered sewage corrupts my way of relating even to those I love the most, let alone my critics. Wretched man that I am! Is there any hope of my forming into a relationally mature follower of Jesus?

Or is it already happening? Is it possible that I *am* on the hard road that leads to life? I read Romans and realize that, with all that is unspiritual within me, I'm in surprisingly good company. Listen to Paul, arguably the most mature Christian who ever lived, talk about his experience as a believer: "I don't really understand myself, for what I want to do is right, but I don't do it. Instead I do what I hate" (Rom. 7:15). As a seasoned Christian, Paul lived with confusion and failure? I can relate. But my confession seems to reach an even lower low. I do what I hate, but in the moment of doing it, I love what I hate. And, to make things more baffling, I hate that I love what I hate.

Let me illustrate, without being inappropriately self-revealing. I could share far worse than what follows. Sarcastic comments directed toward someone I find exasperating make me feel superior, powerful, and closer to those who share the judgment I pronounce on another. And self-righteously retreating from someone who treated me badly helps me feel smugly secure. Too often, without my awareness, expressing love to someone I really do love is driven by a desire to be affirmed that's stronger than my longing to touch the other's heart. Why would I relate that way? I don't want to. Or maybe I do. Learning to love is a battle.

I really don't understand myself. I want to do what is right but too often I do what I hate, and I enjoy doing it before the guilt kicks in. Am I nothing more than an ungodly mess—God's forgiven and well-loved child, thanks to obviously unmerited grace, but still a mess—relationally living like a reprobate who knows little if anything of the Spirit's sanctifying power?

No, I'm more than that. God has begun a good work in me. I am a Christian, and the Holy Spirit is working to form me into the relational pattern of Jesus. And I believe that He will finish the job.

But for now, am I or am I not on the narrow road to life?

Is Sandy? Is she moving toward joy? If not, what direction must she take? Remember Sandy? She's the self-protected woman I briefly described in the prologue. A twenty-year history of significant marital abuse left her traumatized, afraid to risk accepting love from her second husband, whom she knew was a deeply good man. After telling me she feared never being able to love again—had she ever? I wasn't sure—she asked me to pray for her.

Years ago, I might have prayed something like this: "Lord, may Sandy know You feel her pain, that You're with her. And help me to walk with her through her pain to find healing in Your love." Or, had I impatiently descended into a temporary swamp of legalism, I might have prayed, "May Sandy see how sinful she is in the way she relates to her husband. May she repent of her sin, and in the power of Your Spirit choose to love better."

My prayer now was different. "Lord," I began out loud, "Sandy is understandably so aware of her pain and fear that more than anything else she wants to never let anything happen to her that would cause more pain. Jesus, may she believe that You, the Good Shepherd, would lead her onto a difficult path only if it must be traveled in order for her to become the free, whole, loving, and therefore happy woman You saved her to be. And give her both the eyes to see how her protective way of relating is impacting her husband and the heart to realize that she longs to bless her husband at any risk to herself. And lastly, Lord, open her eyes to see You smiling as You look at her, that You're not impatient with her failure to love well, and that You're wanting to release Your Spirit through her to display Jesus-like love. In Jesus's name, amen."

I opened my eyes to see Sandy staring at me. "That wasn't the prayer I expected you to pray," she said.

"Can you say amen to it?" I asked.

She paused, then quietly replied, "I'm not sure."

Is there a narrow road Sandy could walk that would free her to accept that she is loved by God even while she fails to love her husband, a freedom that would then arouse a desire to love and let her discover joy in loving? Is she on that road? Is she even drawn to it? Am I?

Secular psychology provides no help in answering such questions. It cannot adequately define or explain the origin of evil. It cannot fully account for the moral filth that I cannot deny remains within me as I relate to others. And it fails to direct me to a road that will lead me into the delight of being able to truly love well, by divine standards. Psychology cannot reliably guide me or Sandy or anyone else toward the happiness we were created to enjoy.

Therefore, in recent years I have chosen to no longer identify myself centrally as a psychologist. The wisdom I need to recognize what is most wrong with me and the power I need to right my off-course ship must be looked for elsewhere. With only a little hesitation, I prefer now to think of myself as a spiritual director, someone whom I define as a soul companion journeying together with others who share a common desire to know God, to know Him with an intimacy that releases into our way of relating the Spirit's relational beauty, which lies beneath all that is still ugly in our depths.

Embracing that new identity, however, brings into focus a serious shortcoming: *I don't often or reliably experience my relationship with God as intimate.* My aunt Sarah did. When she was a widow in her late eighties, I once asked her what it was like to experience Jesus. She leaned forward and with the passion of a newlywed said, "Sometimes it feels like He's hugging me." Is that a special blessing the Spirit gives to only a few who need that experience, such as lonely, elderly widows? Perhaps a rich experience of God's loving presence is also granted to Christians more spiritually formed than me.

What exactly does it mean to experience God, to believe in Him without seeing Him and therefore to rejoice "with joy that is inexpressible and filled with glory" (1 Pet. 1:8 ESV)? If experiencing God means to fully trust, with felt gladness, in my heavenly Father's heart when mine is breaking, to easily and comfortably rest in the feel-able love of Jesus when I fail or am failed by another, and to gracefully move to the Spirit's relational rhythm when troubles come, then I have a long way to go before I can testify to regularly experiencing God. If you prayed for me as I prayed for Sandy, then asked me if I could say amen to that prayer, at times honesty would require me, with Sandy, to reply, "I'm not sure."

Am I or am I not on the narrow road?

In my sixty-plus years of knowing Christ as my Savior, and relationally sinning every day, I have experienced a handful of times, times that have occasionally stretched into seasons, when I've been reduced to welcome tears, overwhelmed by a deeply felt awareness of God delighting in me, calming all my fears with His love, and rejoicing over me with celebratory music.

But only a handful of times? In more than sixty years?

Shouldn't His delight in me, His love for me, and His rejoicing over me be a more or less continually felt reality? Isn't that the Christian life that mature Christians experience? Isn't that the happiness Christians can know? Must I take my place with immature Corinthians and listen to Paul tell me what he told them? "I had to talk [to you] as though you were infants in Christ" (1 Cor. 3:1). Am I a sixty-year-old toddler?

By classical evangelical standards my theology is orthodox. And yet it's true that I believe truth more than I experience life. But even with my limited experienced enjoyment of the life that gospel truth describes, I am often told that my teaching through books and conferences has made a significantly good difference in people's lives. With all that is still ugly within me, I love my wife and family with genuine and often sacrificial affection. And when someone invites me to speak into their innermost struggles, I feel more gratefully than proudly alive when something comes out of me from the Spirit that makes Christ more real to them. No, I don't believe that I'm a spiritual toddler. I do know something of His joy. I wouldn't describe myself as a carnal Corinthian.

But still an anti-God virus, a strong tendency to advance my felt well-being at any cost to others, remains inextinguishable within me. Yet I long to do right, to bless others at any cost to myself. And sometimes I do exactly that, never purely, but meaningfully. Am I two persons? A double being? Dr. Jekyll one minute and Mr. Hyde the next? The battle to love is real.

I hear the Lord tell me, "I will guide you along the best pathway for your life" (Ps. 32:8). Is that really happening? Perhaps the ugliness and weakness within me is intentionally exposed and somehow dealt with on the path God has me on. Is that the narrow road? Are there stretches on that best path, on the narrow road, that are so dark and troubled all hope of maturity sometimes disappears?

I spoke earlier about spiritual direction, a kind of conversation I've received and sometimes given. But I wonder. Toward what end should spiritual direction aim? Is the Spirit's direction, provided through a Spirit-led spiritual director, supposed to *replace* struggles and failures with a consuming experience of God's intimate presence? Or does Holy Spirit–led spiritual direction somehow awaken and energize the faith we need to persevere on the narrow road when we doubt, to find God's strength in our weakness, to do good though bad still corrupts our efforts, to live with unflagging hope when despair threatens to drown us in futility, to "live thirsty" with a thirst only heaven will fully quench?

The Bible states clearly that God does everything He does for His glory. Perhaps the brightest glory I can give Him comes to life and becomes visible when His Spirit empowers me to reveal by the way I relate both His holy character of love and His sometimes inexplicable but always good ways, even as my internal bedlam continues and at times seems to drown out all noise but its own. It's then that humility is inevitable and dependence becomes necessary. And that's a good thing.

I have a fervent desire to know that I am on the narrow road, and if I'm not then how to get on it. I want to live the abundant life to which the narrow road leads. But a crucial question must be asked: What is abundant in a Christian's abundant life? Many speak of "abundant blessings" in life and "abundant healing" of all our wounds and diseases. For reasons I will later make clear, I believe they are wrong. In this life, neither earthly blessings nor physical healing are guaranteed. When available, they provide only second thing happiness. And that's good, sometimes very good.

But there is something better. Through participation in His life (see 2 Pet. 1:4), made possible through His death and resurrection, Jesus provides an abundance of both the desire and the power to put

His relational energy on display by the way we relate *despite* how others treat us, well or poorly; *despite* whatever seemingly random assortment of blessings and trials come into our lives; and (perhaps most miraculously) *despite* the vile passions, unhealed wounds, selfish desires, foolish ideas, and paralyzing fears that continue to plague us. There's hope for both Mark and Sandy, and for you and me. Abundant relating, loving like Jesus, provides abundant happiness, first thing happiness, a kind of happiness that thrives in a thirsty soul.

Maybe I do qualify as a poster boy for what it really does mean to live the Christian life, the life that's possible now, before we die and Jesus finishes the work of our spiritual formation. Maybe I am living my life on the narrow road, if living on that road means that everything unChristlike within me is slowly exposed and its power to control how I relate is slowly but surely being squeezed out of me. And perhaps, as I walk that road, from my deepest depths the power I need to love a little more like Jesus is being released. Maybe I'm happy with the kind of happiness I don't easily recognize as happiness.

But how does all that happen? What is the narrow road and how does walking on it lead to life?

4

The One Prayer
God Always Answers

No possible degree of holiness or heroism which has ever been recorded of the greatest saints is beyond what He is determined to produce in every one of us in the end. The job will not be completed in this life: but He means to get us as far as possible before death.

C. S. Lewis[1]

A s far as possible before death." Those words have prophetic meaning for me. As I begin writing this chapter, I have been living now for two days with difficult news. The doctor called. Blood test results indicate that the cancer, which surgery has twice before removed, is back.

Is there a narrow road I can walk right now that will lead me to an abundance of life? Will walking that road release me to display to others the relational nature of Christ, the nature now in me that supplies the power to be committed to another's well-being, without pretending that I am feeling what I could only feel if the doctor's news had been good?

By the time you read this, the outcome of my medical situation will have become clear. But now, before the next several months unfold, how am I to think? What am I to believe? Who am I to be? Who *can* I be? Is there a path to follow, a road to travel that will further my spiritual formation, that will actively empower me to advance the plot of God's story by how I treat others, even as I face such an uncertain development? Is that what I want—what I *most* desire—to reveal Jesus to others by the way I relate?

To position ourselves in a praying community, my wife and I have shared the news with friends. I almost said *unwelcome* news. And in a legitimate sense, the news is bad and it is unwelcome. It is neither sinful nor faithless to desire the good things available in this life and to pray for them, including good health. But James, the brother of Jesus, was led by God's Spirit to inform us that troubling news is "an opportunity for great joy" (James 1:2). What did he mean? I would have experienced the considerable pleasure of great relief had the doctor said, "The test came back normal. See me again in a year for a routine checkup." What is the great joy that only comes through great trouble? How is James spiritually directing me to respond today and tomorrow, whatever happens?

Our friends of course will pray. And I am grateful. But how will they pray? How am I praying? What outcome do we most desire? To what end will our prayers be most fervently directed?

When the topic of prayer comes up among Christians, especially when the discussion is provoked by rough circumstances, we tend to divide into two opinion groups. Group 1 folks, with neither guile nor doubt, declare that God answers prayers. We ask, God gives. The only condition is faith. We receive what we believe He will provide. That is group 1 theology. And it focuses people on longing for second thing happiness, the happiness dependent on life's blessings and on physical and emotional healing.

58

When pressed, these sincere believers sometimes acknowledge that on occasion their prayers have seemingly gone unanswered. But an explanation that keeps their theology of prayer intact is quickly offered, usually running along one of two lines: "We may have to wait, but we know God's answer is on the way," or "God knows our heart, so at times He gives us what we really wanted to make our lives better, even though we thought we wanted something else."

Most group 1 Christians give little thought to nuanced explanations for unanswered prayer, preferring to keep things simple. After my first battle with cancer was won through successful surgery, one friend beamed as she said, "I knew everything would turn out well. I prayed that it would." I appreciated her concern for my health, but her words meant little. I prayed for my brother's safe travel on the day he was killed in a plane crash. I don't belong in group 1.

When group 2 believers think about prayer, they lean toward skepticism. They maintain belief in God's goodness and power but they embrace the uncomfortable confusion that mystery requires. For some, a painful history of unanswered prayer has nudged them toward weakened conviction, leaving them to manage circumstances and solve problems as best they can while they loosely follow biblical principles and occasionally throw up halfhearted prayers in case God might be listening and in a mood to respond.

The thoughtful among group 2 sometimes express themselves like this: "We believe in God, we claim Jesus as our Savior and Lord, and we know He cares. We are not deists who believe in a remote and uninvolved God. But prayer as it is often taught in churches makes no sense to us. God is wise and good and powerful, so of course as a sovereign God He does things His way. He needs no counselors to guide Him or spiritual friends to direct Him. He works together whatever happens in our lives toward a purpose that perhaps only in heaven will we recognize as good. It's hard for us to buy into the idea that our prayers can persuade Him to do something He had no intention of doing until we prayed. Mere humans cannot supply

Him with a direction He hasn't considered nor can we offer fervent pleas that He doesn't have the heart to deny, even if granting our request throws His perfect plan a little off course." At first glance, group 2 thinking draws me a bit.

If ever I belonged in group 1, I cut up my membership card when I was ten. It was a Sunday afternoon. In Sunday school that morning, Mr. Von Buchwald had our class looking at Matthew 21:22, where Jesus said to His disciples, "You can pray for anything, and if you have faith, you will receive it." I had never heard that verse before. I immediately signed up for group 1. *Jesus never lies. He is telling me that God will answer any prayer I offer, if I believe that He can and that He will.*

I left church that morning brimming with excitement. After our family Sunday dinner, when Dad retired to his favorite chair with a book and Mother climbed into bed for her weekly nap, I ran outside. I wanted to fly like Superman.

Standing on our driveway, with tightly closed eyes and passionate hope burning in my heart, I prayed, "God, I know You can do anything. I'm asking You to make me fly. I'll jump, and You take it from there."

I did my part. God didn't do His. I jumped several more times, more zealously believing each time that I would soar into the sky. I never flew. From that moment till now, I have never been a group 1 Christian.

But neither have I been able to fit myself into group 2. I believe in answered prayer. Jesus did say that whatever I asked in prayer, if I had faith I would receive it. I cannot deny His words. I believe He meant what He said. But the question must be asked: *What did He mean?*

As I wrestled with that question, another wrinkle in my thinking about prayer occurred to me: Jesus *taught* one kind of prayer and *practiced* another. In the Matthew 21 passage, He guaranteed an answer to whatever we pray for, on the sole condition that we had faith. Believe and receive. That is what Jesus taught. At least so it seems.

But in Gethsemane, He practiced conditional prayer, saying, "if it be Your will" (see Matt. 26:39), which is the kind of prayer with which I am both familiar and somewhat comfortable. "God, here is my prayer. If it is Your will, You will answer my prayer and grant my request. If it is not Your will, You will deny my request in order to accomplish the greater good that is Your will."

Conditional prayer makes sense to me. I don't always like it, but only because my understanding of the greater good doesn't always align with God's. Just as a loving parent, with the greater good of the child's long-term health in mind, denies a child's request to skip the vegetables and enjoy dessert, so God may withhold immediate pleasure that would interfere with an eventual greater good and allow painful difficulties that He knows will advance the good He has in mind.

But what is that greater good? Is it really loving like Jesus so I can be happy like Jesus? Is that what I most want, even if the path to its enjoyment includes something I most certainly don't want, such as cancer? And if in His untainted goodness God is inalterably committed to the greater good, does it follow that every prayer to receive and to delight in that greater good will be answered? What *is* the greater good, for me in this life, to which God is committed? And again I ask, whatever that greater good is, am I certain I want it?

So, then, is Jesus telling us in Matthew 21 that every prayer for the greater good will be answered? If so, then greater urgency is attached to knowing what the greater good is to which God is committed and desiring that good above all others. And in Matthew 26, is Jesus letting us see that any prayer for a lesser good must be offered as a conditional request? "God, I know You *will* my greatest good. If granting my request advances what You are doing in my life, then my prayer will be answered. If denying my request furthers the greatest good to which You are committed, then I gladly surrender to Your will, knowing that whatever troubles You allow to come into my life are irreplaceable opportunities for great joy."

The question remains, and it's important: *What is the greatest good, the good that is greater than all lesser goods?* And when that question is answered, I will find myself at a choice point: Will I commit myself on a daily basis to the good to which God is relentlessly committed, or will I keep chasing after lesser goods that I foolishly desire more, perhaps through prayer? What will I most fervently pray for?

Look more carefully with me at the promise Jesus made to us in Matthew 21:22. The English Standard Version reads this way: "And whatever you ask in prayer, you will receive, if you have faith." Read those words by themselves without context, and a ten-year-old boy's interpretation is warranted. That prayer to fly like Superman should have been answered.

In the next chapter, we will set the stage to examine the context that reveals the meaning of what Jesus said in Matthew 21:22, and in chapter 6 we'll explore that context. And then we can hope to recognize and celebrate the one prayer that God always answers, the prayer my family and friends—and I—are learning to pray with confidence as I face this next battle with cancer. Do I want the greatest good God has in mind for my life, the good that God will work in me if I walk the narrow road? My answer is a still-developing yes. I sense a battle ahead.

5

Am I Even Interested in Praying the One Prayer God Always Answers?

The evil will is still alive even in the followers of Christ, it still seeks to cut them off from fellowship with him; and that is why they must also pray that the will of God may prevail more and more in their hearts every day and break down all defiance.

Dietrich Bonhoeffer[1]

When Christians live their lives on the narrow road, what is it that they most passionately pray for—what do they most long to receive from God? Or put the question this way: What does a "narrow road prayer" look like?

At this moment—I'm scheduled for a CT exam in less than three hours—one prayer has obvious appeal: "Lord, remove whatever cancer may be growing in my body, preferably without using a surgeon's scalpel. I know You *can* do it, and I would appreciate knowing You *will* do it. A guarantee of good health would free me to relax and let me get on with a blessed life I can enjoy." It would be nice if that prayer qualified as one that God promises to answer. It doesn't.

I think Paul would agree. When he was living under house arrest in Rome for the crime of preaching Jesus, no doubt he would have been grateful to receive official word that his sentence had been overturned, that he was free to go. And yet we have no record that he prayed for release from jail. He may have, but we're only told that he prayed for something else.

In a letter to his friends in Philippi, sent from prison, Paul prayed "that your love will overflow more and more. . . . For I want you to understand what really matters, so that you may live pure and blameless lives until the day of Christ's return" (Phil. 1:9–10).

It's clear that what mattered most to Paul was not gaining his freedom from Rome's corrupt justice. His consuming concern was not to enjoy a less difficult, more congenial life. Ask Paul what really mattered to him, and he would answer, "I trust that my life will bring honor to Christ, whether I live or die. . . . I press on to possess that perfection for which Christ Jesus first possessed me" (Phil. 1:20; 3:12).

Two phrases require notice: *to bring honor to Christ* and *to possess that perfection for which Christ Jesus first possessed me*. Whatever those phrases mean, they mattered to Paul. But to our ears so clogged with the waxy noise of culture-bound Christianity, those two collections of words too easily can be heard as religious jargon, sweet pieties that warm our hearts but fail to influence how we relate to each other.

Incarcerate me without just cause and I'd likely chase after what Paul would regard as a lesser good, with no compelling awareness of what he would think "really mattered." Paul prayed for his friends' and his own spiritual condition, that together they would reveal Christ in any circumstance. I fear I would be caught up in demanding the justice I would think I deserved and entreating my friends to secure for me the services of a top-flight attorney with enough connections to bring it about.

And I've done enough marriage counseling (plus been married long enough) to predict that when one spouse offends the other, either slightly or greatly, the offended spouse, whether Christian or not, will cry foul and insist on better treatment, perhaps even calling on God to serve as prosecuting attorney against the offender. The battle then becomes not to love another but to be loved by another.

Broad road prayers most earnestly ask for less than what really matters. Negotiating with God for justice in life or for harmony in relationships are not prayers that reveal a desire for the greatest good. Neither reflects Paul's understanding of what really matters. In Philippians, Paul gives us a glimpse of the sort of prayer Christians pray most fervently when they are living their lives on the narrow road.

I must be careful here. I don't want to be misunderstood. A Christian walking the narrow road, unjustly arrested and now languishing in an Iranian jail, would properly pray sincerely for his release. And everyone who knew of his plight would join in that prayer. And I'm quite certain that an aggrieved husband or wife praying for restored marital harmony would be doing the right thing. God may answer those prayers. Along with my family and friends, I'm imploring God to arrange for good medical news. Each of those prayers is entirely legitimate and God-pleasing, but each is an "If-it-be-Your-will" type prayer. None is guaranteed an answer, at least not the answer prayed for.

Here's the point. If anyone's *lead* prayer, the prayer that reflects their deepest desire, is for positive change in a difficult circumstance or relationship, that person would do well to fear that he or she may be one of the many Jesus followers who are walking the broad road to a wasted life. They do not understand what really matters and therefore never pray the one prayer that God always answers.

I'm concerned, for me and for you. Do we know what really matters? Are we aware of the greatest good we have been freed by Jesus to pray for and pursue, with absolute confidence that our prayers will be answered, exactly as we ask, even while uncertainty continues? Even if we conceptually understand and can articulate what the greatest good is to which the narrow road leads, do we honestly long for that good above all others?

Perhaps I'm so absorbed with "If-it-be-Your-will" prayers, prayers for lesser goods that God does not promise to provide in this life, that, unlike Jesus, I never get around to praying the one prayer God always answers. Perhaps I really don't understand what matters most, in which case I'm ignorant. Or perhaps I know what God defines as the greatest good but still value lesser goods more highly. In that case I'm foolish.

It is entirely possible, and I fear quite common, for followers of Jesus to stroll happily along on the broad road never doubting that they are trekking faithfully behind their Master on the narrow one. Part of the problem may lie with a wrong or at least weak understanding of what the narrow road actually is, and of the greatest good to which it is guaranteed to lead. Are we battling to reveal a better love or to enjoy a better life?

Chuck, the third person I mentioned in the prologue, is clearly in touch with his desire to love better, more like Jesus. But he doesn't see it happening. He's frustrated. "Is there some path I'm missing that would lead to a better love?" he asked.

I hear him asking a how-to question. Like most of us, I suspect he's looking for a formula to follow that would improve the quality of his life by loving better, not a difficult road to travel that would draw him closer to God by loving better. So I answered his question with one of my own.

"Why do you want to love better? Think about it: Are you hoping merely to feel better about how you relate and to enjoy deepening relationships with family and friends? Or do you have a greater motive, to delight God by putting Jesus on display?"

"That second option puts the bar pretty high. I'm not sure I can reach it," he said.

"You can't. Neither can the greatest saint. But there is a road to walk that will empty you of yourself to the degree that you could draw on the Spirit's power, not only to battle for a better love but to actually love better.

"I want to know what that road is, find it, and no matter how narrow to walk through life on it. I want a better life too, but in the center of my soul I want even more to glorify God by putting the way His Son relates on display. But too often, I fall short of that goal. Like you, Chuck, I sometimes find myself preaching (or writing) with more interest in being affirmed than glorifying God. Even then, Christ extends His forgiving and renewing grace, revealing divine love. When I look bad in the presence of that kind of love, I find myself wanting to offer that surprising opportunity to others. Like me, you'll never love perfectly but you will love better. And that's what I'm most praying for. My guess is that's a prayer you want to pray as well."

For years, whenever I heard someone speak of a narrow road that Jesus wanted us to travel through life, two words rather casually came to mind: I was to be *obedient* to biblical principles and I was to *endure* whatever hardships came my way. Obedience, I assumed, would lead to the happy life of blessings that I wanted. And endurance would keep me trusting God's goodness as I confidently waited for the hard times to pass and for good times to return. Walking the narrow road would lead to life, to the good life of the good things I needed to feel good.

I now see that a way of life guided by such an understanding of obedience and endurance is insipid, good-enough Christianity at best and either pharisaical smugness or Laodicean apathy at worst. Of course the Christian life involves both obedience and endurance, but not as ends in themselves and certainly not as the means of winning for ourselves the good life of good times. Important values such as obedience and endurance must be more than chosen duties or manipulative strategies. They must be energized by the life of God within us, the life of love. They must spring from the relationally alive center planted deep in our regenerate hearts that nourishes a desire to reveal the relational nature of Christ to others by how we relate. *That* really matters.

Let me now approach an understanding of the narrow road. Jesus came to tell a story, a love story that could only be told by the way He related to God and to others. Nothing about the way He lived and related comes naturally to us. At best we counterfeit the original way of relating that Jesus brought into this world, living perhaps visibly other-centered lives but with the stain of self-centered motives. Ever since Eden, we are persuaded that there is a better story than God's to tell, one that believes felt self-interest on our terms is the greatest good. Neither the plot nor the point of the story Jesus came to tell resonates favorably with our born nature. We differ with Jesus about what is the greatest good.

Could it be, therefore, that the narrow road is neither a set of principles to obey nor a series of difficulties to endure but is rather a story to tell? And could it be that it is the plot of that story that makes the road narrow? The plot of the story Jesus came to tell and intends to continue telling through us, mostly through how we relate, runs exactly counter to the plot of the story we are naturally and stubbornly committed to telling.

The narrow road is a path that takes us precisely into the battle between the two stories, between our will and God's will. (How it does that is for later chapters.) Each storyline is relational. Each tale is a love story. One story centers on an unwavering commitment to the well-being of others at any cost to ourselves, with no *entitled* concern for either the justice we desire or the comfort we want. That commitment reveals the heart of God and engages us in the battle for love.

The other story draws its storyline from a stubborn commitment to our well-being at any cost to others. We relate to others for our sake. That commitment reveals our fallen heart, the energy source of all that goes wrong in our relationships. The wrong story, authored by Satan and attractive to our self-centered nature, calls us to battle for fair treatment, to have things go our way, to enjoy the good life of blessings and healing. The story Jesus came to tell discloses God's love for us. The story we insist on telling is centered on our love for ourselves.

There are two opposing stories, each one being told in the life of every Christian. The clash of the two stories is the narrow road, creating tension in a Christian's soul that uncovers our core desire to tell the story of Jesus.

The Christian walking the narrow road fights a daily battle between these competing stories. Failure is inevitable. But where sin leaks out, grace floods in, putting us more deeply in touch with our love for the grace-filled Jesus and with our desire to tell His story to others by how we treat them. There is little question—the broad road offers a more comfortable journey through life, and for a simple reason: *only one story, the wrong one, gets a hearing on the broad road.* The core value is self-interest. The core identity of the traveler on the broad road is an independent self, not a relational soul. The image of the relational God is blurred, eventually to the point where divine relationality disappears from sight. How I treat you isn't the point. What matters is how you treat me and how life treats me.

Broad road believers feel entitled to a blessed and therefore happy life, a life preoccupied with enjoying second thing blessings. They sense little tension from wrestling against a difficult and wearisome storyline that promises to yield the greatest good. "If-it-be-Your-will" prayers enjoy priority on the broad road, fueled by the assumption that God's priority is to provide us with the satisfying circumstances and pleasant emotions we most desire, or at least with some relief from pain.

Life on the broad road is popular among group 1 Christians, those who take for granted that prayers for the good things of life are dependably answered. Should unanswered prayers drive some into group 2, where people resign themselves to serving an undependable God, folks lose interest in looking for a prayer that God always answers and remain on the broad road, hoping to not mess up their lives too badly before they reach heaven.

I belong in a third group. I *don't* believe that I can decide what is good for me and then count on God to provide it. And although sometimes I do, as a pattern I *don't* retreat into cynicism over a God so far above me that He remains unresponsive to my good. I *do* believe that God will grant what a long walk on the narrow road convinces me really matters and stirs me to desire above all lesser goods.

There is a prayer God always answers. Jesus said so in Matthew 21:22. "You can pray for anything, and if you have faith, you will receive it." Jesus meant what He said. He always does. *But what did He mean?* A look at the context that led up to that promise of guaranteed answer to prayer reveals the one prayer God always answers, the prayer for our greatest good that will only be asked and answered on the narrow road.

6

Our Deepest Hunger, Felt Most Deeply Only in Emptiness

> When [John of the Cross] finally gave expression to his relationship with God, the first word was a bewildered cry exposing a raw wound—a world outside John's control where the only certainty was his hunger.
>
> Iain Matthew[1]

There is a prayer God always answers. It is a prayer, I'm slowly learning, that I express most intensely when I'm feeling my emptiness most acutely. What exactly is that prayer? Listen to the story that was unfolding when Jesus told us there is a prayer God always answers.

In the morning, as Jesus was returning to Jerusalem, he was hungry, and he noticed a fig tree beside the road. He went over to see if there were any figs, but there were only leaves. Then he said to it, "May you never bear fruit again!" And immediately the fig tree withered up.

The disciples were amazed when they saw this and asked, "How did the fig tree wither so quickly?"

Then Jesus told them, "I tell you the truth, if you have faith and don't doubt, you can do things like this and much more. You can even say to this mountain, 'May you be lifted up and thrown into the sea,' and it will happen. *You can pray for anything, and if you have faith, you will receive it.*" (Matt. 21:18–22)

That is the passage. And it tells a story, a brief incident in the life of Jesus. Look with me now at the story to better understand what was happening in Jesus when He told His disciples, and us, that there really is a prayer that God always answers.

It was early morning. Jesus had just spent the night in Bethany, a village about two miles from Jerusalem. The day before He had left Jerusalem after enraging the Jewish leaders by overturning the money changers' tables in the temple courtyard. And now He goes back. He returns to the city where He knows crucifixion awaits. We can safely assume, I think, that the dreaded event was on His mind, and that He was walking to Jerusalem with a strong sense of destiny. In speaking about the Messiah's impending death, Isaiah tells us that He set His face "like a flint" (Isa. 50:7 ESV), resolved at any cost to tell the story He came to tell, a story about to enter a brutal chapter in which the torture would be severe enough to surprise even Him. His mind was on the story, both its extreme difficulty and its dazzling outcome.

As He walked along the road, He spotted a fig tree. Mark adds the significant detail that the tree was "in full leaf" (Mark 11:13). In Israel, fig trees do not usually sprout leaves until early summer, or at least not until late spring. Jesus was heading toward Jerusalem in *early* spring. A tree in full leaf got his attention. He was hungry, as anyone would be setting out on a hike without having eaten breakfast.

Mark's version of the story clearly suggests that Jesus thought it possible that early leaves might indicate early figs. "He noticed a fig tree in full leaf a little way off, so he went over to see if he could find any figs" (v. 13). Nothing is wrong with wanting a legitimate but lesser good, like breakfast.

But Jesus found only leaves and no figs. Now remember what was most on Jesus's mind: He was about to die so that human beings who brought no delight to His Father could become a pleasure in His sight. At that moment, when He realized that the presence of leaves suggested the availability of figs but obscured their absence, Jesus, I assume with obvious vehemence, spoke to the tree: "May you never bear fruit again" (Matt. 21:19).

I understand that Jesus was disappointed when He found no figs beneath the leaves, much as I am when a waitress serves me lukewarm coffee. One would think Jesus might have said, "Oh well," and moved on. The absence of figs was only an inconvenience, not a tragedy. But Jesus cursed the tree, and immediately every leaf withered.

The disciples were with Jesus. They saw what happened and they heard His angry response. If they had had no inkling who He was, if they had thought Him only a buddy, they would have seen Him as peevish, rather immature and petulant, and perhaps would have chided Him. "C'mon, Jesus. It's no big deal. You had a home-cooked meal last night. We'll have breakfast in Jerusalem. We'll be there in less than an hour."

But they knew He was no mere mortal, so, I think awkwardly, maybe sheepishly, they asked, "How did the fig tree wither so quickly?" (v. 20).

Have you noticed in the Gospel accounts that from our perspective Jesus answers questions poorly, if at all? One would have thought Jesus might smile and offer a rich comment about His limitless power. I imagine His disciples were caught off guard when instead Jesus replied, "I tell you the truth, if you have faith and don't doubt, you can do things like this and much more" (v. 21). Was Jesus actually telling them that with faith they could move about the country and wither leaves on fig trees? Literally, no. But figuratively, yes.

Remember where in the Bible fig leaves are first mentioned. After Adam and Eve sinned, "they sewed fig leaves together to cover themselves" (Gen. 3:7); in other words, to present themselves before God while keeping their failure out of sight. They were hiding behind fig leaves, hoping to conceal from God's eyes that they had no fruit for Him to enjoy.

In Hosea, the Lord laments over His faithless people. Like a father who remembers his son as a delight in younger years, though now the son is a drug addict, "The LORD says, 'O Israel, when I first found you, it was like finding fresh grapes in the desert.'" Then He shifts metaphors. "'When I saw your ancestors, *it was like seeing the first ripe figs of the season*. But then they deserted me for Baal-peor, giving themselves to the shameful idol. Soon they became vile, as vile as the god they worshiped'" (Hos. 9:10).

Notice the obvious. *Neither Adam nor Eve nor Israel in Hosea's day had any fruit for the Father to enjoy.* Adam and Eve hid their absence of fruit, or at least tried to. The people of Israel had no convicting awareness of their failings. Like the Jews in Jeremiah's time, "they did not know how to blush" over their abominations (Jer. 6:15 ESV).

Jesus knew He was about to die. But He was also aware that only those who shed the leaves of pretense and stood naked, blushing with shame in the presence of a holy God, owning that nothing about them deserved kindness, would gain the supreme advantage of the death Jesus would soon suffer. I suggest that when Jesus saw fig leaves and no figs, He was reacting to more than a lost opportunity for breakfast. He was deeply distraught by the realization that people all around Him were leafy trees with no fruit, refusing to confess their heinous failure and their desperate need for a Savior. I hear Jesus telling His disciples to wither their fig leaves, to stop displaying themselves as better than they are and, with divine power, to encourage everyone they meet to do the same.

He then added, "You can even say to this mountain, 'May you be lifted up and thrown into the sea,' and it will happen" (Matt. 21:21). Did Jesus mean what He said? Of course, but again figuratively, not literally. Had Peter turned toward the hill Jesus pointed to and told it to jump, move, and fall into the nearest body of water, would it have happened? Unlikely at best.

Remember Isaiah's prophecy when he looked over barren Israel—God's people who were bearing no fruit for God to enjoy. Think of all that stood in the way of their spiritual formation into fruit-bearing disciples: ungodly leaders, hardened hearts, false worship, disappointment with God. Yet Isaiah had faith. "A great road will go through that once deserted land. It will be named the Highway of Holiness" (Isa. 35:8). But mountains would block progress on that road. So five chapters later, Isaiah wrote, "Make straight in the desert a highway for our God . . . *and every mountain and hill be made low* . . . and the glory of the LORD shall be revealed" (Isa. 40:3–5).

As He anticipated crucifixion, I hear Jesus declaring with great passion that no obstacle will be allowed to stand in the way of disciples who walk the narrow road to life, who own their relational sin and pursue no greater good than relational holiness. Narrow road Christians long to bear figs for their Father to enjoy. And if that's what we most want, Jesus guarantees it. That guarantee supports Jesus in His happiness.

Can I put it this way, without even a hint of disrespect? I hear Jesus on a roll, like a fired-up preacher so excited about what's possible because of Christ but deeply distressed over people who aim too low, over disciples who don't long as their top priority to bring honor to Christ by the way they relate to an unloving spouse or a rebellious child or a betraying friend or an insensitive pastor, over professing Christians who don't want to press on to possess that perfection for which Jesus first possessed them, the perfection of loving like Jesus and displaying His love by how they relate to others.

I hear Him saying something like this:

I am going to Jerusalem for one reason, to die. My death will clearly and powerfully and forever tell My Father's story of love, His plan to form people into disciples of Mine who would continue telling My story by the way they relate to others.

I envision prodigals returning to My Father's home and enjoying a feast of relational blessings that will empower them to bear relational fruit. The leaves of self-deception and pretense will wither and fruitless followers will depend on My Spirit to produce fruit. Everything that stands in the way of that story—abusive parents, sexual addiction, unfaithful spouses, heartbreak over children, prolonged unemployment, feelings of insignificance, loneliness, depression, everything difficult in their lives—will not be permitted to block My followers from learning to tell My story.

I want My followers to enjoy confidence that they can ask for withered leaves and lowered mountains, for *anything* that furthers My story, and if they trust Me to complete the work I died to begin, they will slowly and with much patience learn to tell My story well, by relating like Me.

I met Greg when we were both on vacation. When I introduced myself, Greg paused for a moment as if trying to remember something, then without enthusiasm said, "I've read some of your books." Before I could respond with a humbly appreciative comment, he asked, "Do you still believe everything you wrote?" His question felt less like an inquiry and more like an attack.

I decided to answer honestly. "I have struggled with my faith, at times almost to the point of giving it up. But I've come to a place where I believe that whatever the Bible affirms is true. And to the degree that my books reflect its message, which I hope is considerable, yes, I still believe what I've written."

Another pause, then Greg said, "I don't believe any of it anymore. I used to believe, but no longer."

"What happened?" I asked, assuming that, as with other former believers I've known, some tragic event had taken place in his life that he couldn't square with his Christian faith. My two-word question unleashed a lengthy reply. Here's the condensed version.

"My older sister was the godliest Christian I ever knew. When a college professor got me questioning the whole Christian thing I was raised to believe, she was the one, not my parents, who kept me believing. Thanks to her my faith survived that crisis. But then she got cancer. She was thirty-four, happily married with three young kids, and she died within six months of diagnosis. I had prayed every day that she would live. I can't worship a God who says He's good and then treats one of His best followers like that. Either He doesn't exist or He isn't good. I'm done with the whole Christian business."

It's always true that unless God's Spirit opens someone's eyes, they remain closed. Sometimes that truth is obvious. This was one of those times. A quote from Oswald Chambers floated into my mind: "The root of all sin is the suspicion that God isn't good." With that thought stirring in me, I said something like this to Greg.

"It's taken more faith than I thought I'd ever need to keep believing God is good and in control of what happens. At fifty-one, my older brother was killed in a plane crash. Later, my dad lost my mother to a seven-year battle with Alzheimer's. Through all that and more, I realized the faith I needed had more to do with trusting that God is telling a good story even when bad things happen, and that in all the really hard stuff God is moving everything toward a good purpose that I can see now as good and will fully enjoy only later."

"I've heard that line before," Greg said. "I memorized Romans 8:28 in Sunday school."

"Me too. That verse only makes sense to me when I see that the good purpose is not only forgiveness for being so self-centered but also that somehow God uses suffering to free me to actually care more about someone else than about myself," I said. "And that freedom does something in me that I really like. I pray for protection from things I don't want to happen, but I pray with confidence that He'll protect me from getting even more self-obsessed as a victim and free me more to tell His story of forgiveness and hope by how I relate to people. And when I do, I know what the word *joy* means no matter what else is going on in my life."

"I still don't buy it," Greg said. "I wish I could. Well, thanks for the chat. Maybe I'll see you around."

We shook hands and he walked off rather slowly, perhaps wondering if there might be a prayer for something he deeply wanted even more than his sister's restored health, a prayer that God would answer.

There is a prayer that God always answers. It is this:

Make me like Jesus, a little Christ who puts Him on display by how I relate.

That's the prayer that comes with a guarantee from Jesus Himself. It is the prayer to be spiritually formed—*relationally* formed—to advance the plot of God's story, the gospel of Jesus Christ, in every relational encounter. Nothing matters more. It is the greatest good. And it leads to the truest joy available in this world, the happiness Jesus knew when He lived here.

God's Spirit has begun this great work in my life, and in yours if you've trusted Him to give you life. How He intends to continue that work is my focus in the rest of this book. Our part is to know what the narrow road is, to find it, and to walk on it till we walk forever on the streets of gold. Only on the narrow road will the Spirit form us to live and love like Jesus, to share in His suffering and to taste His joy. But there's a big problem.

7

Who Am I?

Dr. Jekyll? Mr. Hyde? Both?

I had long been trying to write a story on this subject, to find . . .
a vehicle . . . for that strong sense of a man's double being which
must at times come in upon and overwhelm the mind of every
thinking creature.

Robert Louis Stevenson[1]

I stood already committed to a profound duplicity of life . . . the
personal war among my members . . . man is not truly one, but
truly two . . . I learned to recognize the thorough and primitive
duality of man.

Dr. Henry Jekyll[2]

I sometimes experience myself as two persons in one body, two
collections of emotions and thoughts striving against each other.
Just last night, I lost sleep by angrily worrying over a friend who

was poorly handling a difficult situation in his life and, at the same time, I was aware of a surviving confidence that God was at work in this godly man's heart. The internal dialogue between two opposing forces is rather unsettling. The urge to escape the tension and smother the worry by watching television or eating a cookie is strong.

I know myself to be a committed Christian, a man who truly wants to delight, honor, and reveal Jesus by the way I live my life and relate to others. More than once, many times more, I have wept with anticipated joy as I have imagined myself actually meeting Jesus and hearing Him say, "Well done, my good and faithful servant" (Matt. 25:21).

I'm reminded every day, however, that all within me is not well. A felt concern that God will not do what I believe needs to be done, especially in my life and in the lives of those I love, releases a surge of desire to experience a measure of peace-giving and pleasurable distraction by doing something I know will grieve and dishonor Jesus and will then obscure Jesus by the way I subsequently relate to others.

In these moments I feel torn. It seems as if my soul is split in two. I don't, even for a moment, want to turn my back on the One who loves me as no one else can. But I come up against a powerful competing force. I recognize an opportunity to feel a kind of quieting relief and satisfying rest that Jesus doesn't seem to provide, an opportunity to experience a pleasure so strong that seizing the opportunity feels, well, perhaps not so terribly wrong.

The battle is on. The trap is set. And sometimes it snaps and catches me, and I sin, most often by how I relate. I snub someone or impatiently snip at them. The options are many, and each one in the moment feels delicious, or at least necessary and therefore justified.

Relational sin presents itself to the offender as less heinous and more easily excused than behavioral sin such as adultery or violence. Don't all of us guard ourselves at times and find more happiness in hurting less by protecting ourselves more? Maybe that kind of relating distorts the true meaning of love, but it seems necessary to our well-being. Is it really so bad? The answer is yes.

Sinning by how we relate falls shamefully short of the way our three-Person God relates, and it creates pain and distance in our relationships that never exist within the divine community and were never intended to exist in ours. The harm I cause when I relationally sin ruins, at least for a season, any hope of life-giving connection with others. By judging, ignoring, demeaning, or patronizing others I allow nothing of the intimacy the gospel makes possible to develop in my relationships. What foolishness!

Relational sin, I suggest, is a way of sinning to which every Christian must plead guilty. It has the power to destroy marriages, parent-child relationships, friendships, and ministry effectiveness among colleagues as effectively, though perhaps more slowly, as adultery, abuse, or betrayal. Only those blind to both the motives beneath their way of relating and their impact on others will, wrongly, plead innocence.

I want to love others. I want those I love to feel loved, to taste through me the love that Jesus so freely and fully pours into them. And yet I relationally sin. Am I two persons?

Behavioral sin, often involving sexual wrongdoing, is another category of evil. Men often see themselves as morally clean if they have never committed adultery and if they only rarely sneak a peek at pornography. Their assertion of purity requires that they not take seriously the Lord's teaching that "anyone who even looks at a woman with lust has already committed adultery with her in his heart" (Matt. 5:28). The immoral beast of self-centeredness that warrants and drives self-satisfying rebellion against the standard of God's relational purity is in all of us, more obviously expressed in some than in others.

For example, a Christian friend whom I'll call Tony struggles to control the urge to look at pornography, an urge that occasionally and with no obvious prompt swells within him. He sometimes yields.

And yet he meaningfully loves Jesus and truly hates sin. To borrow Robert Louis Stevenson's phrase, my friend experiences himself as a "double being." He longs to do right, and usually does. But at times the desire to do wrong feels stronger. At those times, the desire to do right cannot seem to successfully compete with the desire to do wrong.

Why? Isn't Tony, like every other Christian, a partaker "of the divine nature" (2 Pet. 1:4 ESV)? And don't we all have a Holy Spirit–created new heart that with supernatural power yearns to do right (see Ezek. 36:27)? Why, then, does Tony's desire to do right (and too often mine) feel weaker than his desire to do wrong?

Two reasons. First, the urge to click on a porn site rises up from a passion-filled center, a center that feels entitled to feeling good when one feels bad. *The sinful urge comes from a place within Tony that he experiences as a deeper place than his redeemed soul.* That's one reason, grounded entirely in subjective experience.

The second is more objective. It's this. *Sin delivers a pleasure that Jesus never provides*, a pleasure that fills the self with nothing that can be lovingly given to another and therefore, in the middle of experienced pleasure, it makes joy impossible. (Remember: in my terms, first thing happiness is the same as joy.) This pleasure—a form of second thing happiness—is self-gratifying, a kind of delight that inevitably ends in the misery of loneliness but for a short time feels wonderful. We must reckon with the rarely stated truth that sin brings with it an experience of consuming pleasurable satisfaction that holiness never supplies.

In order to compete with sin's appeal, holy desire, the longing to live a Christlike life that displays the relational beauty of Christ to others, must be rooted in faith. And that faith exists only when it is lodged in the certainty that soon it will give way to an incomparable experience of joy that will forever destroy the appeal of sin. As later chapters will show, that faith only develops on the narrow road. The journey requires an ongoing battle between competing stories, a battle that can yield first thing happiness now.

The question remains. Is Tony a double being, two persons in one body, each person competing for dominance? Am I? Is every one of us a Dr. Jekyll, a decent and good person, and at the same time a Mr. Hyde, a beast lying in wait within us for the opportunity to indulge without immediate penalty whatever God-hating, self-loving desire promises a kind of self-satisfying delight that yielding to God-loving, self-denying desire never dispenses? My answer is no, we're a different kind of double being. Let me explain.

You've heard of Dr. Jekyll and Mr. Hyde. Perhaps you've read the book. Written by Robert Louis Stevenson and commonly regarded as a classic, *Dr. Jekyll and Mr. Hyde* tells the story of a deeply troubled physician relishing the freedom to give way to his base instincts and hating himself when he does.

The book hints at autobiography. Stevenson became aware of himself as a double being in the religious culture of a Scottish Presbyterian home. Raised in the mid-1800s by a religiously devout and demanding father and a hypochondriac mother who panicked whenever little Robert had the sniffles, he learned a distorted version of Christianity from his nurse Cummy, a hired woman who spent more influencing time with Robert than his parents. Today we would call Cummy a right-wing religious fanatic, a caring nurse who was at the same time a fire-and-brimstone extreme fundamentalist. Among many other radical views, she taught Robert that "the theatre was the mouth of hell, cards were the Devil's Books and novels"—romance novels—"paved the way to perdition."[3]

Stevenson survived adolescence and entered adulthood believing there were only two possible ways to live: to *be good and scared*, always worried that you weren't good enough to avoid hell, or to *be bad and happy*, numbing your fear of judgment by living however you pleased.

Given his background, it's likely that as a child Stevenson was familiar with Romans 7. If he was, he probably saw himself in Paul's self-description as a kind of double being, a man torn by competing appetites. Paul put it this way: "I have discovered this principle of life—that when I want to do what is right, I inevitably do what is wrong. I love God's law with all my heart. But there is another power within me that is at war with my mind. This power makes me a slave to the sin that is still within me" (Rom. 7:21–23).

Paul experienced himself as a battlefield where a war raged between two antagonists, two inclinations within him that were inalterably and fiercely opposed to one another. And too often he found himself giving in unstoppably to the evil force. That accounts for his lament: "Oh, what a miserable person I am! Who will free me from this life that is dominated by sin and death?" (v. 24). I cry out in similar agony when I sin, relationally or behaviorally. So does Tony.

Paul went on to state what Tony and I long to declare with greater evidence and appreciation. "Thank God! The answer is in Jesus Christ our Lord" (v. 25). I hear Paul saying there is a happiness available that puts an end to a certain kind of misery, a kind of happiness available not in more blessings but in Jesus.

It seems that Stevenson failed to find in Jesus the answer to his intense battle between two persons. Could it be because he had not accurately perceived who those two persons were? In his loosely autobiographical novel, Stevenson has Dr. Jekyll mixing rare chemicals into a potion that when swallowed freed him from the narrow constraints of a moral life and released him to enjoy without guilt the pleasures Mr. Hyde felt when he indulged his monstrously evil desires. When the potion wore off, Hyde disappeared and Jekyll returned, overwhelmed by how strongly he "hated and feared the thought of the brute that slept within him."[4]

The novel's final chapter consists of one long letter written by Dr. Jekyll to a close confidant, a letter in which he somewhat defensively but very miserably revealed his life as a double being. His closing words record a conclusion that no Christian need ever reach.

> Here then, as I lay down the pen and proceed to seal up my confession, I bring the life of that unhappy Henry Jekyll to an end.[5]

I've briefly reviewed the broad themes of both Stevenson's life and the story he wrote for one purpose. I think Stevenson had it wrong. And many Christians, at times including me, share his disastrous misunderstanding of what it means to live in this world as double beings.

In Stevenson's understanding, Jekyll's existence as a double being left him with only two dreadful options. Either he could live a morally decent but hollow life, always struggling with the allure of pleasure that only wickedness could bring, or he could throw caution to the wind and freely indulge whatever impulses promised to deliver a kind of delight that morality never provides.

What is the old saying—close but no cigar? Paul's understanding of what it means for a follower of Jesus to live life as a double being was perhaps similar to Stevenson's on the surface but in reality was quite different. He acknowledged that a beast lives in even the most devoted and spiritually formed Christian, but he also recognized the devilish source from which the beast drew its life. The battle was against God's enemy and the Satan-like nature that the fall in Eden created in our core.

Happily, Paul celebrated the truth that Jesus came into this world on a rescue mission that no Special Forces unit could ever pull off. He came to write a wonderful story that forgives us for telling a terribly bad story in which self-interest is featured, a story about Dr. Jekyll searching for a feel-good freedom that only Mr. Hyde could enjoy, a freedom to do terrible things that Dr. Jekyll hated but wanted to do.

That same story of Jesus, Paul realized, empowers Jesus followers to tell a truly good story in which divine love, the kind that finds purpose and joy in sacrificing self-focused desires for the sake of another, expresses itself in even the worst of circumstances and relationships. And it energizes and sustains the storytelling expression of divine love by bringing into view the certain climax of eternal joy in loving community released in a perfect world.

If we forget Christ's story or misinterpret it to mean that our greatest good in this world is the good life of blessings that stir good feelings, we become "little Jekylls." We travel on the broad road of required morality that provides more pressure than joy, thinking that following God's rules brings God's blessings, the blessings we determine we need to enjoy our lives.

When the formula doesn't work, when we live well and life gets hard, or when a life of blessings leaves us with a deep ache in our souls (as it inevitably does), we degenerate into "little Hydes," victims of our own misery who feel compelled to make whatever choices bring at least relief and hopefully pleasure. We then yield to urges that promise a kind of satisfaction that Jesus never gives.

I am a double being. So is Tony, and so are you. But we are not Dr. Jekylls fighting a losing battle against Mr. Hydes. As does every Christian, I live as a developing "little Christ" and a determined "little devil." In the gospel story we are new creatures, not obligated by fear of death to be good, but designed and desiring to live a new way, a way that fills emptiness with hope, that defeats frustration with purpose, that rules over futility with meaning, and—best of all—that arouses a divinely given desire and power to love like Jesus, even in the midst of betrayal's sting or disappointment's anguish or failure's guilt or inadequacy's discouragement or isolation's loneliness. The narrow road to which the gospel story leads us releases the joy of *knowing* love that *frees* us to love.

The devil's story is disguised by the world as compulsively appealing if not especially good, and its plot draws on our spirit of entitlement to justify doing whatever we must to feel freedom from struggle and to experience whatever satisfaction we can generate.

The double being of a Christian—a little Christ freed to tell the great story of God that delivers the greatest good available to us now, and a little devil who settles for pride-enhancing, independence-building, and self-satisfying pleasure that eliminates relational intimacy—walks the narrow road that exposes the ugliness and utter foolishness of Satan's story and reveals the beauty of Christ's story and strengthens the faith required to tell it. It is on that road and no other that each little Christ will slowly win many battles against each little devil, until final victory is eternally won.

We're almost ready to explore more fully what the narrow road is and how its narrowness does the work of relationally forming us to put Jesus on display in our communities. Life on the narrow road is God's plan for our spiritual formation. His plan isn't easy, but it's good. And it's always successful in the end.

Who am I? Dr. Jekyll? Mr. Hyde? Both? No, neither! Like you, if we're both walking the narrow road, I am a slowly forming little Christ who will not be ultimately defeated by the little devil that still too often gets the best of me. And that's good news.

8

A Passion for the Impossible

Adherence to Jesus allows no free rein to desire unless it be accompanied by love . . . therefore a will dominated by lust can never be allowed to do what it likes.

Dietrich Bonhoeffer[1]

Humanly speaking, it is impossible. But not with God. Everything is possible with God.

Jesus Christ[2]

I want to follow Jesus. I want to more fully know what it means to be His disciple, to follow Him on the narrow road to life. Writing this book is compelling me to realize there is more to a "narrow road life" than our Christian culture commonly understands or believes is necessary, and there is more involved in walking that road than I have come to grips with and personally absorbed, even after all my years of identifying myself as a follower of Jesus.

I shouldn't be surprised. Of course there is more to living life on the narrow road than I have yet recognized or appreciated. Through His Spirit, God is committed to making me holy as I follow His Son. No day passes without something reminding me that the goal is still a long way off. Do I yet understand what makes the narrow road narrow and how its narrowness squeezes unholiness out of me? Maybe my understanding will grow if I think more carefully about the requirements for being a disciple of Jesus. Perhaps they remain unmet. Could that account for my too often shallow happiness that too easily gets nudged aside by some level of misery? Perhaps there is another dimension to the battle for a better love that I have not yet meaningfully considered.

Luke records a revealing incident that took place when Jesus was having dinner at the home of a Pharisee. A large crowd gathered around Jesus as He seized the occasion to teach. Apparently they were open to becoming His disciples, to learning from Him what life was all about and how to live it well. What He said to them is curious; it's also surprising.

I would have thought that the One who invited all who were weary and sick of religion to come to Him might have warmly welcomed them as followers, perhaps saying, "So good to see your interest in who I am and what I have to offer. I'm glad you're here, so now we can start walking together on a wonderful journey through life."

But instead Jesus turned to them and pointedly said, "If you want to be my disciple . . . don't begin until you count the cost" (Luke 14:26, 28). Apparently, Jesus wants intelligently committed followers, not shortsighted admiring fans.

In the next two chapters, we'll carefully look at the specific cost Jesus told them to count. My focus now is this: *I hear Him saying these same words to me.* I'm to count the cost of true discipleship before I excitedly promise to follow Him come what may. An emotional decision is one thing. A thought-through commitment is quite another.

But I've been a Christian now for more than six decades, to all appearances and with some reality a meaningfully determined disciple. Is there more to the cost I have yet to count? Are there depths of surrender I have yet to experience? Perhaps Jesus wants me to know that there is never an opportunity, when walking the narrow road, to coast—to rest, yes, but never to coast. Until I see Him in the next world, I must not assume that all is well within me, that any further changes need only be cosmetic.

There is always a higher cost to count and a richer life to live. Any who think otherwise, who are blind enough to believe they have fully counted the cost and paid it, have chosen an easier life on the broad road. They make little impact on others. A failure to count the cost weakens a Christian's power to count for Christ. I must *continually* count the cost if I want to be an authentic disciple of Jesus who becomes a little Christ.

But there is a problem. Jesus obviously intends that I take seriously His instructions to count the cost. Of course. But when I do, I'm initially neither encouraged nor excited. I feel defeated. Let me briefly list now (and later discuss) the three costs of discipleship that Jesus mentions in Luke 14:25–33. One, I'm to hate everyone but Jesus, including myself. Two, I'm to deny my natural desires at every turn and walk through life carrying a cross. And three, I'm to renounce all claim of ownership to everything I possess.

Is He kidding? He might as well ask a pauper to come up with a million dollars. I can't do it! *And maybe that is precisely what He wants me to realize, to confess that I can never check "counting the cost" off my to-do list.*

I did not begin writing this book with a well-worked-out set of ideas that I wanted to teach you about what it means to live your life on the narrow road. I rather began with questions I felt were important enough to explore, and as I do so I'm feeling a few familiar truths coming freshly alive in my mind. The fog is lifting from two truths that I'll mention now, truths that arouse my desire to count whatever cost I must if I'm to walk the narrow road.

The First Truth

In the hidden center of my soul, I long to enjoy the greatest good that Jesus makes available in this life to all who count the cost and follow Him.

Let me put it more simply: *I'm thirsty.* I'm thirsty for God more than I'm thirsty for Him to do good things for me, like curing my cancer and seeing to it that it never comes back. I want that too. But I want God and the greatest good He makes available to me more than I want anything else. Anything else is less. I'm not always aware of a burning desire to surrender to His greatest good for me, but it's always there, lodged in what the Bible calls my "inward being" (Ps. 51:6 ESV), what in new covenant language we can refer to as our "new heart."

Like a deer pants for water, from depths I cannot easily access, I want God. From those same depths I can sometimes hear myself groaning as I cry out, "When can I go and stand before him?" (Ps. 42:2), or as *The Message* puts it, "I wonder, 'Will I ever make it— arrive and drink in God's presence?'" I can't always hear that cry pouring from my inner parts, but I believe it's always there.

Until the day I meet Jesus, God's Spirit is continually awakening my desire to know Jesus well enough to put Him on display in my world by how I relate to others. I long to love like Jesus. The Spirit is working to make that my ruling passion. Father Zossima, the spiritual director in Dostoyevsky's great novel *The Brothers Karamazov*, defined hell as the suffering of being unable to love. If Zossima was right, and I believe he was, it follows that heaven is the delight of being able to love, the freedom to fulfill our destiny as little Christs.

In always increasing measure, that delight and freedom is available now as a preview of what eternally lies ahead. And notice this: when Jesus commands us to love, He is actually issuing an invitation to experience God, *to know His presence by revealing His nature.* I long to respond to that invitation. The desire for God's greatest good lies deep within me, whether at any given moment I feel it or not. That is the first truth I'm right now seeing more clearly. The desire is in me to love as a disciple of Jesus.

The Second Truth

I cannot pay the cost that I must count in order to live my life as Christ's disciple.

I'm simply not strong enough, good enough, or surrendered enough to meet His terms. I've understood this before, but today the truth of my weakness seems less well disguised. The great cost reveals the strength I lack, my utter inability to pay the price. Remember the cost: hate everyone but Jesus, keep every desire in check that is not motivated by love, and relinquish all title to everything I own.

In her last days of life, Mother Teresa was struggling. After decades of never experiencing the joy of Christ's presence (but knowing a different kind of sustaining happiness) and now suffering a painful death process, she cried out, "Jesus, You're asking too much." She paid a dear price to follow her Lord, and it seemed too much. I look at the cost Jesus is asking me to count, and from the comfort of a considerably blessed life, with far less reason than Mother Teresa, I groan. *He's asking too much.*

Yes, I am thirsty. I do want what Jesus offers. I've taken Him up on the free gift of forgiveness, a guaranteed spot in heaven, and a relationship with each member of the Trinity. But now I realize there is a high cost to living the life I've freely received. It's too high. I can't pay it. I'm not certain I'd want to if I could. It requires something so unnatural: hating family, denying desires that yearn for satisfaction, holding on to nothing I possess.

Why? Why does Jesus insist on a cost I cannot pay in order to enjoy what I most long to receive? As I wrestle with this question, it becomes clear that my inability to pay the price has much to do with weakness but more with stubbornness. As this second truth registers, I realize it isn't simply that I *can't* pay the price, it's that I *won't* pay the price. And I come to grips with the dismal awareness that self-centeredness and unbelief make up the sin that still "dwells within me" (Rom. 7:20 ESV).

I see that all hope of being fully spiritually formed before I die will be unrealized and that a claim to "have no sin" (1 John 1:8 ESV), to think that the pure heart now in me, thanks to the new covenant, always releases pure love with no corrupting self-interest mixed in, means that I am fooling myself, that I'm self-deceived and "not living in the truth" (v. 8).

As Jesus lays out the cost of following Him, I hear Him letting me know that I must drown in the inevitable failure of Romans 7 before I dance in the joyful freedom of Romans 8, that I will celebrate the beautiful heart of Jesus only to the degree that I agonize over the wretchedness in mine.

I read the words I have just written and I want to wail—*God, the cost of discipleship is too high!* It crushes me. It exposes my poverty and pride. And it all seems so dark, so depressing, and so unnecessary for living a decent, normal, pleasantly blessed, and gladly generous life. I know God wants more for me than a good-enough Christian life, which isn't a richly spiritually formed life at all. But I'm having trouble feeling the deepest desire I know is in me, the desire to walk the narrow road that promises to free me to love like Jesus.

But as I wail, something unexpected happens. The painful awareness of weak desire and stubborn resistance and inevitable defeat gives way to a hopeful thirst I couldn't experience before. An entirely unreasonable urge rises within me, bubbling up through all my weakness, resistance, and defeat—*a passion for the impossible.*

I can't stop wanting what I can't afford, *and I can't stop believing it's available.* Grasping both truths—that I thirst for what will only come to cost-counting disciples and that I can't, I won't, pay the required cost—leaves me feeling alive, free, and full of hope. It makes no sense. I can only explain what happens as the mysterious and miraculous work of the Spirit, a work of grace that leaves me happy.

Isaiah's words come alive with new hope. Speaking for God, the prophet asks, "Is anyone thirsty?" (Isa. 55:1).

And I cry out, "Yes! Me!"

Isaiah continues, "Come and drink—even if you have no money!" (v. 1).

"Lord, I'm bankrupt. I cannot pay a dime."

Then God urgently but calmly responds, "Listen to me, and you will eat what is good. You will enjoy the finest food" (v. 2).

I'm not sure I understand. But with absurd hope, I long to love like Jesus, *and I believe I will,* even when I'm angry, when I'm lonely, when dinner guests talk too much and stay too late, when life deals me one unfair blow after another, when my family life hits some big bumps, when friends disappoint me, when illness creates frightening uncertainty, *and* when I realize how unlike Jesus I relate. In any circumstance of life, in any condition of soul, I long to love like Jesus.

Here's the point: *the impossible becomes possible when I follow Jesus on the narrow road.* Part 2 of the book explores how that happens. But know this now: the narrow road is as long as the years of your life. More miles stretch before me, as they do before you; perhaps many, perhaps few. Either way, every failure as we walk that road presents a new opportunity to be stunned by the gospel, to look bad in the presence of love. Somehow, it is the truth of God's story, a story centered in amazing grace, that can free us to love like Jesus. *It's possible,* never perfectly till heaven but richly now.

What I'm learning as I write this chapter is this: our passion to walk the narrow road, aroused by both our thirst to love and to be loved when we fail, makes room for the Holy Spirit to do what He most longs to do. It's His specialty—to make possible the impossible, to stir in Jesus followers our God-given desire and power to put Jesus on display by the way we relate to others. In this life that is our greatest good, the source of our deepest joy: the God-delighting pleasure of knowing Him and making Him known.

But how does all this happen? Look with me now at the three-part cost Jesus presented to would-be followers two thousand years ago. It's a cost that must be counted—notice Jesus never said it must be *paid*—if we're to understand how living life on the narrow road frees us to know Christ well enough to love like Him, to satisfy our passion for the impossible.

9

Freedom to Follow

Freedom in the light of hope is the creative passion for the possible. . . . The person who is a servant of the Most High is . . . completely free from other things and other powers. He fears God alone and nothing else in the world. He belongs to the Lord and no one else.

Jürgen Moltmann[1]

Jesus began His teaching ministry by first, in no uncertain terms, letting us know what is most wrong with us, and then, only then, telling us that something unspeakably wonderful is now available to us. After emerging unscathed and uncompromised from a forty-day wrestling match with the devil, though no doubt exhausted, a resolute Jesus started to preach.

"Repent of your sins." Sin is your biggest and worst and most lethal problem—not social injustice, not poverty, not homelessness, not unemployment, not cruel tyrants, not sex trafficking, not physical disease, but sin—*your* sin. "And turn to God, for the Kingdom of Heaven is near"—the relational kingdom of My Father and I and our Spirit; become citizens of that kingdom and an entirely new way to relate to others in this often disappointing, unfair, hurtful, sometimes devastating, and always corrupt world will open up before you (see Matt. 4:17).

Not long after that opening gambit, Jesus preached His longest recorded sermon, which we know as the Sermon on the Mount. In that sermon, He carefully and in great detail laid out an untried way to relate with people, a way that comes naturally to no one and makes sense to few. Toward the end of His revolutionary teaching in that sermon, Jesus firmly warned His listeners, "the gate is narrow and the way is hard that leads to life, and those who find it are few" (7:14 ESV). In those words, I hear Jesus telling me that following Him does not promise to open the door to good times but rather to hard times for a good purpose. The battle is on.

After a few more thoughts, the sermon ended, and "the crowd burst into applause. . . . This was the best teaching they had ever heard" (vv. 28–29 MSG). It soon became clear that the clapping crowd had no idea what He was talking about, no clear idea of what it meant to live their lives on the narrow road.

Just like today. I've often been one among many who rose to their feet in energetic appreciation for a powerful message about what it means to follow Jesus, and later realized I'd heard what I wanted to hear and blocked out whatever required more of me than I was prepared to give. It's a rough road that leads to real life. That's what Jesus said. Have I heard Him? Or have I settled for a faint facsimile of what it means to be His disciple?

Most everything Jesus says in the Gospels surprises me before it draws me. He *couldn't* be saying what makes me so uncomfortable. His teaching reliably catches me off guard, but, when I'm listening to learn, it nudges me to not back away in confusion or discouragement but to keep studying and thinking, to ask His Spirit for wisdom to grasp and receive the radical teaching. In my search for wisdom, I realize again and again that His ways are far above mine and His thoughts are not thoughts I would come up with on my own.

The more I study Christ's hard words, the more I become gladly dependent on Bible-grounded, Spirit-guided dialogue with Jesus and His followers, and the more my interest wanes in dotting every i and crossing every t to arrive at dogma about the way the Christian life works that with imperious authority I can then pass on to the less-well-informed Jesus followers. Instead, I want to remain open to wherever dialogue with God through His Word, His Spirit, and His people takes me, hopefully to humble convictions that can guide my way of relating, not to proud certainties that I can impose on others.

Too often, though, the surprising and difficult words of Jesus push me away from resting in His truth. Doubt slides toward irritability. Rather than deferentially waiting for clarity to come, I am led by my impatience in one of two directions. Either I'm tempted to interpret Christ's words to better fit what I want Him to say or, if I recognize how disastrous such a course of action would be, I find myself easing past what I neither understand nor like and comfortably settling on words that on their face seem more agreeable—an equally disastrous course.

Let me quickly illustrate that second bad option. In the upper room shortly before His crucifixion, Jesus told His disciples, "The Father himself loves you dearly because you love me and believe that I came from God" (John 16:27). Good! I like that thought. I love Jesus. I believe He came from God. I can now count on God's love to give me what I need to enjoy life, blessings such as cured cancer. That's what loving fathers do for their children, if it is in their power. My heavenly Father certainly has the power. Blessings, the ones I want, will follow. How easy it is to twist Jesus's words into a guarantee that things will turn out as I want them to, to leave the narrow road and travel on a broader one.

Let me now offer one example of words spoken by Jesus that rattle me and make little sense on the surface. Think with me as I work my way into the untidy clutter of confusion. Dealing with this clutter might help us later to profitably engage with the Lord's teaching about finding real life by walking on, and staying on, a rough road. Those words have been rattling around in my mind and soul for some time and have prodded me to write this book. Let's wrestle with them, with no demand for a clear understanding of what Jesus was saying. Sometimes admitted confusion opens our minds to unexpected wisdom.

Jesus was on a speaking tour. After preaching in several towns to crowds of listeners who seemed attentive but were cautiously skeptical and proved to be obstinately unpersuaded, Jesus did something I wouldn't have expected. He *thanked* His Father for hiding the truth He was presenting from so many of the people, from those who were "wise and clever." You can read about this incident in Matthew 11:7–30.

Was Jesus *grateful* that so few believed Him? I'm aware that proud people, the wise and clever folks today who have Christianity and the Christian life pretty well figured out, listen to their preachers not to learn what they don't know but to confirm what they already know. They have little interest in teaching that questions their convictions, that unsettles their complacency, or that calls them to a new way to relate when they are already quite satisfied with how they are relating.

As someone who has delivered many messages over the past forty years, I empathize with pastors who feel discouraged, who struggle with personal inadequacy or frustration with people when truth they present from the pulpit reaches very few in the pews. A paralyzing sense of futility more than once has diminished my desire to ever again preach a sermon or lead a conference. *Is anyone really listening? Am I even listening to what I so confidently declare?*

But to thank God for seeing to it that people listen to truth without hearing it? I would have thought Jesus might plead with His Father to send the Spirit to humble all the know-it-alls, to open their eyes rather than closing them more tightly. And yet He thanked God for keeping His ministry unsuccessful. That surprises me. And it doesn't draw me. It's not easy to warm up to either the Father or the Son when their way of doing things so obviously differs from how I think things should be done. (Think ahead for a moment. A hard road to a good life? I'd arrange things differently.)

Then Jesus goes on to again thank His Father, this time for revealing the truth of His message only to the "childlike." Apparently, Jesus was okay with God blinding the eyes of the many and giving sight to the few. Listen to what He said: "Yes, Father, it pleased you to do it this way!" (Matt. 11:26). Why? Why did it please the Father to not bless His Son's ministry in ways we might expect? And why was Jesus thankful for an unresponsive audience?

Turning to the crowd who had been eavesdropping on His puzzling prayer, Jesus then says something that couldn't have made sense to them. "My Father has entrusted everything to me. No one truly knows the Son except the Father, and no one truly knows the Father except the Son *and those to whom the Son chooses to reveal him*" (v. 27).

Two thousand years later, after reading the other three Gospels and the rest of the New Testament as well as the Old, I hear those words and I think I get more than what His original audience understood. But an important question remains. *Jesus, why don't You reveal the Father to everyone? Couldn't You humble the proud, embrace the childlike, and enlighten them both? Will You, eventually?* Universal salvation has its appeal.

I want Jesus to reveal to everyone who God is, a community of overflowing love, and to make known the breathtaking plan He has in place for our release from sin and misery; and if not to everyone, at least (selfishly speaking) to everyone I love. Among others, five grandchildren come nervously to mind. Many of my friends, and countless other Christians across the world, live every day with broken hearts over loved ones who remain stubbornly unimpressed and blithely indifferent to the story Jesus is telling. And prayer, passionate and unceasing, seems to make no impact on God. I'm thinking it may require a long walk on the narrow road, whatever that means, before the truth of God's sovereignty becomes cause for gratitude.

I'm not only puzzled by what Jesus says, I'm worried. Is it possible that I'm one of those who thinks himself wise and clever, so settled and sure of how I've come to understand the path to spiritual formation that I'm not open to new or different understandings drawn from Scripture? Will I interpret what it means to live my life on the narrow road in a way that lines up with what I want it to mean—and in the process will God hide from me what Jesus means? To put it differently but no less alarmingly, am I free to follow Jesus when the narrow road becomes narrow in a way I thought it never would, when it becomes so narrow that something I strongly value is being squeezed out of me—something, for example, such as good health or a grandchild's embrace of the gospel?

Am I childlike enough to continue traveling on the only road—the narrow one—where the story of Jesus reveals both the stupidity and the arrogance of the story I prefer to tell, the one that I so easily believe has a better plot? As the narrow road squeezes out of me what I've long believed I cannot live without, will brokenness over my foolish narcissism release a cry for mercy from my soul? Or will I grumble and complain, and tenaciously hang on to whatever remains that seems essential to my well-being? If I'm truly childlike, the story of Jesus, after throwing me off balance, will draw me upward into the beauty of Trinitarian community and to God's beautiful but costly plan to reproduce through me that kind of community in this world. That is what I want. And it will bring happiness.

In the same Matthew passage, after unsettling me with what He already has said, Jesus shifts gears and seems to contradict Himself.

He now invites me, and everyone else who is confused and troubled, to enjoy Him. "Come to me, all of you who are weary and carry heavy burdens, and I will give you rest. . . . Let me teach you . . . and you will find rest for your souls . . . *and the burden I give you is light*" (Matt. 11:28–30).

But as we've already seen, in the Sermon on the Mount Jesus clearly stated, "*the way is hard that leads to life*" (7:14 ESV). One notable scholar translates that same phrase this way: "how rough the road leading to real life."[2]

Which is it? Will I find rest for my soul as I carry the light burden Jesus gives me? Or will the road to real life be a rough go? Can both be true?

I hear the Lord's invitation, and I respond. I come to Jesus, telling Him I am weary, weary of failing, weary of life, weary of trouble, and weary of religion. A rough road carries little appeal. I want rest. I want soul rest, to carry only light burdens as I learn from Jesus what it means to live "the new way of the Spirit" (Rom. 7:6 ESV).

I pray, *Jesus, I want to follow You, to live the rest of my life as Your committed and passionate disciple.* He hears me, He pauses, and then I hear Him say:

> If anyone comes to me and does not hate his own father and mother and wife and children and brothers and sisters, yes, and even his own life, *he cannot be my disciple.* (Luke 14:26 ESV)

This is a "light" burden you're laying on my back? Is this part of the narrow gate I must cram myself through to get on the hard road? But I love these people. And You told me in another place to love them, especially my wife, and even my enemies. And now You're requiring me to hate the people I most love before I can walk the narrow road of discipleship? I don't get it. And I don't like what I understand You to be saying.

He goes on.

"Whoever does not bear his own cross and come after me *cannot be my disciple*" (v. 27 ESV). Luke also records another time when Jesus added a phrase to a similar requirement. "If anyone would come after me, *let him deny himself* and take up his cross daily and follow me" (9:23 ESV).

Have we, today's Christians, not heard the demands of Jesus? Have we ignored the requirements for becoming His disciples, or perhaps heard but then dismissed them? Have I?

Jesus, You set the pattern. You denied the deepest desire of Your heart, which was to never experience the loss of intimate togetherness with Your Father. Were You in touch with an even deeper desire? And You denied Your sinless desire to not suffer the shameful humiliation and excruciating agony of crucifixion. Jesus, Your cross was not light. It was heavy.

I gather I'm to follow Your pattern. But what does it mean for me to deny myself? I sometimes skip dessert and feel like a martyr. What cross am I to carry? Will it be heavy but feel light? Did Your heavy cross somehow feel light as You stumbled beneath its weight? That makes no sense. Your cross was heavy. The burden Your Father gave You was not light. But I'm to believe that if I walk the narrow road, the burden You give me will be light?

I'm not sure I understand what You're telling me. I'm quite sure I don't. What I'm hearing You say, Jesus, seems more confusing than appealing.

Then Jesus adds the third cost I must count if I am to follow Him on the narrow road: "Any one of you who does not renounce all that he has *cannot be my disciple*" (14:33 ESV).

Is Jesus contradicting what His Spirit inspired Paul to later write? The apostle told Christians who could afford to own a lot of this world's goods *not* to give everything away but rather to not trust their wealth and instead to trust God "who richly gives us all we need for our enjoyment" (1 Tim. 6:17).

So I assume, Jesus, that You're not telling me to sell my house, give all the proceeds to the poor, and live on the street. And You don't necessarily want me to give away my car and walk wherever I need to go. What then do You mean when You tell me to renounce all that I have? I'm confused and again not especially drawn to Your words.

But I want to be! I know that Your ways and thoughts, though bewilderingly above mine, are good. I know You well enough to trust Your heart, that Your plans for me "are plans for good and not for disaster, to give [me] a future and a hope" (Jer. 29:11). And, can I say, to make me happy?

I want to walk the narrow road, to follow You as Your disciple. But I read that three-part cost of discipleship and I wonder—what does each one mean?

A woman in her late thirties, Beth, became familiar with this teaching through me.

"You're making it seem too hard to follow Jesus," she said. "I got saved when I was fourteen. And God has blessed me with all kinds of good things. Why can't I just be happy with the good life God has given me, stay involved in my church, and enjoy doing all I can to be a good wife and mom? If I got into following Jesus by counting those three costs, I think my husband would believe I've become a fanatic. It would probably put some distance between us. And I don't want that."

I replied, "None of us, including me, is going to count the cost of true discipleship that Jesus laid down unless four things are true in our lives: one, that we believe Jesus meant what He said, not as an option but as a command; two, that we understand what He said and believe what He meant; three, that we're more interested in glorifying God than leading a comfortable life; and four, that because He loves us, we know He'll never tell us to do anything that would get in the way of what we were created to enjoy."

With a grudging smile, Beth said, "Sometimes I wish I'd never met you. I'm just not ready to count that cost. I'm not sure I even know what it means to do what Jesus said."

"Beth, until you see that all you can bring to God in the hope of becoming who you're meant to be is your failure, weakness, and thirst, you'll see the Christian life I'm talking about as an effort you can't manage. When you come to Jesus with a lot of self-centered sin that you know no effort can overcome, you'll then discover the freedom of grace, the pressure-free joy of looking bad in the presence of love. Then walking the narrow road will be something you'll want to do.

"But if you come to Him with your good life, with your faithful church involvement, and with your good wife-ing and mothering, then you'll be living to get on God's good side so that He'll bless you and you'll feel entitled to His blessing. Beneath all the good you do, you'll really be performing to win approval. And that misses all the joy of the gospel of grace."

Beth was living what I call the good-enough Christian life. There is nothing supernatural about such an existence. Without Jesus, people can enjoy blessings and live responsibly, even generously. But ongoing denial of their God-created, image-bearing desire to radically and dangerously love is required to stay happy as a good-enough Christian, with second thing happiness.

Perhaps you are wondering, along with me, what these three costs of discipleship mean and what it means for us to take them seriously—what it means to count them. In the next chapter, I'll offer some provisional answers to these questions, answers that might open the door to the narrow road, to enjoying our freedom to follow Christ on a rough path to real life, and to actually experience our burdens as light.

From a deep place within me, I pray that together we will experience freedom that in the light of the hope guaranteed to us by Jesus will release from our minds and hearts the creative passion for what was impossible but now, thanks to the unfolding story of God, is possible—to become like Jesus in how we relate to the Father and to others, by the power of the new life within us, a divine life created in us and released through us by the Spirit. It's time to dance with the Trinity as people who share God's nature. *We are free to follow Jesus.*

10

Three Faces of Entitlement

> There is no real life apart from the knowledge of Christ. . . . It
> is as we yield our wills to Him that we enter the strait gate and
> pass into the narrow way that leads to life—life in its richest,
> fullest sense—to be embraced in measure here on earth but
> enjoyed in all its fullness in a blest eternity.
>
> H. A. Ironside[1]

I first thought to title this chapter "Preparing to Walk the Narrow
Road." But it occurred to me that these words might miscom-
municate my intent, suggesting perhaps that followers of Jesus are
to do something akin to walking a pirate ship's plank, bound and
gagged, with no hope of survival.

Then again, that may be my exact intent. Let me explain.

The Death Wish

Every true follower of Jesus has somewhere within them, perhaps
in a very hard to reach place, a compelling and life-loving death

wish. Jesus did. It's unmistakable—Jesus *wished* Himself to die. No one took His life from Him. Willingly and freely, certainly not painlessly—can we say gladly?—He laid down His life. He chose to walk the plank to a horrible death.

But why? Why would He do such a thing? Had He become hopelessly discouraged with a failed ministry? Of course not! Jesus never has failed and never will fail at anything He sets out to do. He wished Himself to die in order to live again with a life He could pour into us, a kind of life that survives death, that emerges only after death; the kind of life every self-aware person longs to be able to live, the life the Trinity has been enjoying for a long time, a deeply happy life. His dying served an eternally good purpose. As can ours.

Paul, too, had a death wish. After meeting Jesus he determined every day to die, to walk the plank of death to self. Paul eagerly wished to die to every desire that, if indulged, would get in the way of his Christ-won opportunity to really live. For him, really living meant to *enjoy* God above every other possible source of delight, to *enjoy* giving himself to others in soul-nourishing relationships, and to *enjoy* advancing the great purpose for which he lived, to tell the greatest story he had ever heard. Paul prayed to die to every power that pressed in to control him other than the power of God's Spirit.

In this chapter, I want to explore a Christian's death wish, our Spirit-generated desire to die to what I'm calling the three faces of entitlement. Together, these expressions of an entitled spirit represent the desires alive in all of us that, if we're to become disciples of Jesus, we must be eager to kill. When Jesus laid out the three-part cost that would-be disciples must count, He was revealing to us the spirit of self-serving entitlement that shows its ugly face in each of our lives, usually on a daily basis.

Here is the point I want to make in this chapter, right up front: *we prepare to walk the always narrowing road to always deepening life by becoming aware of what it is we want to kill and how it is we long to live.* Jesus wants to help us discover our death wish, our yearning to die to everything that robs us of the joy that no suffering or pain can eliminate.

Notice this; it's important. Most often, we discover our good death wish and feel its strength *after* we enter through the narrow gate into relationship with Jesus and *before* we trust our very souls to Jesus by stepping onto the narrow road. Christians commonly, and I believe wrongly, assume that once through the narrow gate that serves as the birth canal into God's family we are without delay ushered onto the narrow road that carries us toward maturity.

But something important needs to happen between the far side of the gate into new life and the onramp to the narrow road where we are positioned to be spiritually formed. Paul appealed to "brothers," to folks he knew to already be Christians, to do something essential to becoming genuine disciples. He urged them to *present their bodies as a living sacrifice to God and to His kingdom story* (see Rom. 12:1). Every Christian is called to martyrdom, to die for the cause of Christ, to die to everything that gets in the way.

There is a cost to discipleship, a cost that is poorly understood and watered down in much of today's Christian culture and too often in my own life. The cost must be understood in all its severity before it can properly be counted and before we will live on the road to spiritual formation. Count the cost and you're on the narrow road. Don't count it and you're not. It's as simple and unbending as that.

Between getting through the narrow gate and getting on the narrow road there is a space, a gap of opportunity. It is graciously true that the moment we receive the double gift of forgiveness and new life in Jesus, a new appetite rises up within us, a longing to know God that resides in our hearts with greater strength than any other appetite. It is that appetite for God that begets our death wish, our desire to die to anything that gets in between our God-thirsty souls and our soul-satisfying God. *But the desire to live for God and to die to sin, though alive in our regenerate souls, often remains only weakly felt if felt at all.*

And that is a tragedy. Here's why: no one walks the narrow road without experiencing the twin desires that exist in the soul of every Christian. Only those who become aware of a compelling desire to know God at any cost to their pride and comfort and who discern within themselves a hatred for whatever obscures the reality of His loving presence will find themselves on the narrow road to life.

Think of the gap between "getting saved" and "becoming a disciple" as a vestibule, a kind of hallway with one door opening into a living room. This living room, however, is not what one might expect. Peek through the door—it's always ajar—and you will see that this living room is more like a long, narrow road that invites onlookers to move toward an unseen destination, a destination that somehow you intuitively know you want to reach.

Peek again and this time you see only enough light to illuminate the first step into the road-like living room and the barest outline of sparse furnishings. Only a single bench is visible. This is a room in which we're to *live*?

The hallway is different. It is brightly lit and spacious, with comfortable chairs scattered generously throughout, each one inviting occupants to rest. Your choice becomes clear: step into the dark, narrow living room with one hard bench, an option that promises to lead you toward a good place, or remain in the hallway and enjoy immediately available comfort. The second option seems better. It is, however, the devil's deception.

As you weigh which choice to make, if you listen closely you will hear the voice of Jesus: *Don't be fooled. The hallway is the broad road. Settle there and you will lead a wasted life. The living room is the narrow road. Travel through it and all that is self-centered within you, all that corrupts your efforts to relate well, will eventually be exposed as worthy only of death.*

You are already alive with My life, with supernatural passion to sacrifice everything for My Father's glory and for the advancement of His relational kingdom in people's lives. But you are not yet free to care about anyone's well-being more than your own.

Come, be My disciple. Enter the living room. Die to yourself and walk the narrow road to life, the relational life that I displayed for thirty-three years when I lived in your world and most visibly displayed during the three years before I died. And nowhere was the relational glory My Father gave me more fully revealed than on Calvary. It is that glory I now give you.

But know this: you will experience no sustaining power to walk the narrow road into relational life until you discover your desire to love Me as your only source of real life and until you perceive that you do hate all that comes between us and are therefore willing to turn away from all of it.

We prepare to travel life on the narrow road by counting the cost of discipleship. Simply put, the cost is a willingness to die to everything that competes with our desire to live—to live and love like Jesus.

Look with me now at the severe-sounding three costs that must be recognized and counted if we're to become spiritually forming disciples of Jesus. Keep in mind that the cost is usually counted *not* as we enter the narrow gate but after we pass through it and before we resolutely set foot on the narrow road. Would-be disciples must confront these demonically hideous faces of entitlement that disguise themselves as friendly but always obscure the beauty of Christ. Many of us, I fear, have yet to recognize these three faces in our lives and confront them.

The Threefold Cost of Discipleship

Cost 1: Hate Everyone but Jesus

In our Lord's words:

> If anyone comes to me and does not hate his own father and mother and wife and children and brothers and sisters, yes, and even his own life, *he cannot be my disciple.* (Luke 14:26 ESV)

111

What on earth does Jesus mean?

In each of our lives, two stories are being told, each one vying to be the one spoken through our lives. The unholy trinity—the world, the flesh, and the devil—is consistently telling a very bad story, that, though pleasant for a time, has a very bad ending. And yet I can still find the pleasant chapters appealing, a clear indication that I have not yet fully seen the incomparable beauty of Jesus. Happiness from blessings can draw me more than happiness from holiness, the holiness of loving like Jesus.

In one version of the bad story (and there are many), I might follow a Christian-looking script by turning to God for the blessings and healing I need to enjoy the good life and to which I feel entitled as a member of God's family. The script then calls for me to turn away from God and turn to people—spouse, parents, children, friends, pastors, colleagues—for the love, respect, and support I believe I must have if I'm to feel good about myself and my life, to enjoy a healthy sense of self-worth, and to rest content in my circumstances.

And that represents the point of the bad story, the climax to which the bad story promises to lead: *me enjoying me in a pleasant life*. According to the script, Jesus is granted a supporting role. He becomes useful—perhaps even necessary, like an attentive waiter in a fine restaurant—to the outcome which the bad story assures me I'm entitled to enjoy. I remain the star, the coddled hero of the bad story. And I arrange my life in order to experience second thing happiness.

But think how the plot unfolds. I "love" my family and friends for what they can give me, for what I need from them to feel valuable, worthy, wanted, admired, and respected. It is that perversion of love that constitutes the first face of entitlement: *I depend on you for what I most need*. It is the devil's version of love, a wicked counterfeit that is nothing better than disguised selfishness.

When this first face supplies the energy with which I engage others, I bring a me-centered agenda into each relationship:

- Come through for *me*.
- Take *me* into account, my fears, my insecurities, my painful history.
- Treat *me* well, as I define well.

Our holy Lord sees our badly twisted understanding of "love" and responds by telling us to "hate" everyone, to hate everyone but Jesus *as the source of what we need to reach our God-glorifying goal*, to live for Jesus and to love like Jesus. That's the goal of the story the holy Trinity is telling, the good story.

Family and friends can hurt us deeply but they can never destroy us. Family and friends can meaningfully love us but they can never provide the life we need to love like Jesus. At their best, they stir up the love God's Spirit has already provided. The divine life lodged in the center of our souls is indestructible and is sufficient to move us along the narrow road to becoming more Christlike. How foolish to embrace the goal of the bad story, a solid sense of self-worth, and to then depend on others to help us reach it. How stupid to gorge on the junk food of people's approval that provides only a fragile sense of personal value when the rich food of God delivers the imperishable reality of security and dignity into our souls, both realities undeserved but gratefully received and enjoyed.

Let me put it differently. Only when we *reject* everyone but Jesus as the ultimate source of living water for our thirsty souls will we be free to see others as opportunities to put Jesus on display, no matter how they relate to us. It is in that sense, and in that sense only, that we are to "hate" everyone but Jesus.

The first cost I must count requires that I see the first face of entitlement grinning at me and clobber it. I must be willing to depend on no one but Jesus in order to tell the good story with my life. I certainly should gratefully value and be nourished by what my Christian community gives me, but I must radically depend on God's

Spirit to tell the story that scripts me to shine the spotlight on Jesus as I make His beauty visible by how I relate to others.

Cost 2: Deny Yourself and Carry Your Cross

In our Lord's words:

Whoever does not bear his own cross and come after me *cannot be my disciple.* (Luke 14:27 ESV)

And he said to all, "If anyone would come after me, *let him deny himself* and take up his cross daily and follow me." (9:23 ESV)

There are two elements that make up this second cost to count, that together reveal the second face of entitlement that must be mutilated: *self-denial* and *cross-carrying.* Consider self-denial first.

"Let Him Deny Himself"

It is obvious that every person comes into this world thirsty not only for physical water to keep the body alive but for spiritual water, living water that is necessary for the soul to live. We bear the image of a social God, a relational God whose way of relating defines the life He enjoys in His three-Person community. Though often with little or no awareness of it, each of us is thirsty to relate with His passion.

He is happy. And we were created to be happy, like Him. As finite image-bearers we long to fill our empty souls with the satisfaction that comes only when we learn to relate to each other with divine love. As fallen image-bearers, however, we look for satisfaction in another way, through people who love us and respect us as worthy to be loved and respected. We've turned away from Jesus.

But no one other than Jesus can be counted on or is able to provide what we were created to experience. So now we're afraid and angry. Suppose no one loves us as we long to be loved. Our fear of living life unsatisfied perverts our legitimate desire to be satisfied into a self-focused demand to be satisfied, a demand that someone other than God satisfy our thirsty souls. And that requirement becomes the second face of entitlement: *I demand to experience satisfaction through you.*

This second face smirks with a deceptive delusion. The satisfaction available through someone or something other than God is only the illusion of a complete meal. Ask any sex addict. In the moment of pleasure, and only for that moment, the addict feels fully satisfied, fully whole in the satisfaction experienced, desiring nothing more. That experience plays into the devil's hands. Why? *Because the satisfaction God gives His followers is never more than a taste, a very good taste to be sure, but only a taste of the banquet yet to come.*

Our choice then is this: wait for the complete satisfaction we trust is coming, or experience now what convincingly seems to be complete satisfaction. For Paul, our choice is clear: to "groan inwardly," knowing the best is yet to come, and "wait eagerly" for the abounding satisfaction we wish we could feel now (see Rom. 8:23 ESV).

But that is difficult to do. Our presently felt dissatisfaction, our legitimate longing for more, reliably converts our desire for satisfaction into a demand. And opportunities to yield to that demand are rife.

It is reprehensibly natural for us to begin every day by laying claim to our assumed right to feel what we long to feel. The second face shows itself in many ways. Let me list three that shape our everyday attitudes:

- I want to feel good. That is a legitimate desire, a desire to feel happy, but I demand that it be satisfied in my time and on my terms.
- This thing (sex, success, food, possessions, drugs, alcohol, recognition, money, or ministry) provides a kind of satisfaction I can experience in no other way. I therefore demand it. I deserve it.
- It is only human to want satisfaction. It is not wrong to be human. So, it follows that whatever gives me that satisfaction

is not wrong. I demand my right to feel good about me and my life. There is nothing sinful about that demand. I want to be happy!

But a demanding spirit *is* sinful. In the presence of a holy and generously loving God an arrogant demand to feel satisfied *is* shameful. Jesus requires that we deny ourselves the immediate satisfaction we demand in order to better savor the tastes of His goodness now, a different kind of happiness that whets our appetite for what is soon coming at the banquet of joy.

"Bear His Own Cross"

Each disciple-to-be must also "bear his own cross." The phrase is familiar to most Christians. But I fear its meaning has been commonly misunderstood. The cross we must carry if we follow Christ is *not* defined by what we normally think of as suffering. Of course everyone runs into some kind of trouble, but not everyone contracts cancer. Not every marriage fails. Not every loved one dies prematurely. Not every business or ministry falls apart. Not everyone battles depression or disabling anxiety.

But everyone who loves suffers. God suffers because He loves. He created us in order to love us. But He suffered beyond what we can imagine when Adam and Eve, believing a better offer was on the table, rejected His offer of friendship in the garden. Jesus suffers too. Though He suffered horribly on the cross, very few if any readers of this book will suffer the agonies of crucifixion. Neither, I expect, will its author.

And yet we're told we must suffer *as Jesus suffered*. What did Paul mean when he insisted we must "suffer with him in order that we may also be glorified with him" (Rom. 8:17 ESV)? And what on earth was Peter talking about when he declared that we are to "rejoice insofar as you share Christ's sufferings" (1 Pet. 4:13 ESV)? If neither Paul nor Peter meant the suffering of actual crucifixion, what suffering did they mean?

My answer? *Relational suffering, the suffering of unrequited love.* To feel what Jesus must have felt when, looking over the holy city where His chosen people lived, He lamented, "O Jerusalem, Jerusalem . . . How often I have wanted to gather your children together as a hen protects her chicks beneath her wings, but you wouldn't let me" (Luke 13:34).

Jesus suffered relationally. His disciples will similarly suffer. Real love will inevitably meet with a disappointing response in a world full of relationally sinful people, people like me who demand that others provide the relational satisfaction we crave. A disappointing response to love is inevitable—not always, but often. And it hurts.

Unrequited love, the searing heart-pain every loving disciple will suffer, is the cross every loving disciple must carry. And when that cross is laid on our backs, we are sorely tempted to off-load it. Divorce the insensitive spouse. Marry another or play it safe and remain single. Retreat from or get even with friends who fail to return your kindness. Stick with the ones who appreciate all you do for them. Defend yourself against the others.

Jesus says *no!* Instead, deny yourself. Do not demand others come through for you. See everyone as an opportunity to display the love of Jesus. And carry your cross. When you do your best to sacrificially love another who treats you poorly, perhaps even with contempt, suffer with Jesus. He knows exactly what you're feeling. Rejoice to the degree that you share Christ's sufferings, because He longs to enjoy your company as together you hurt, but continue to love, and together anticipate the eternal day of perfect community. Count the cost. Walk the narrow road. Learn the suffering of love. It will deepen your fellowship with Jesus, and it will form you to love like Him.

Cost 3: Relinquish the Title to Everything You Own

In our Lord's words:

Any one of you who does not renounce all that he has *cannot be my disciple.* (Luke 14:33 ESV)

117

If Jesus is not telling us to own nothing, and He is not, then what is He requiring of us in order to get on the narrow road of discipleship? Peter points us toward the answer: "Dear friends, I warn you as *'temporary residents and foreigners'* to keep away from worldly desires that wage war against your very souls" (1 Pet. 2:11).

Today's Christianity tends to focus on improving living conditions and quality of life in this world. In the process, we devote more energy to making a better world than growing better people, *relationally* better people who display Jesus in their primary relationships. We often live as though primarily we are citizens of this world: advancing social justice, restoring health to the sick, reducing the divorce rate, and generating prosperity that will make many lives more secure and comfortable.

All the above are worthy endeavors and are God-honoring and kingdom-advancing. Christians should be leading the way in each of these things, *but not as our first priority*. Remember Christ's prayer to His Father shortly before He died. Notice what was most on His mind: "I pray that they"—all His disciples—"will all be one, just as you and I are one" (John 17:21). As an outcome of His terrible death, His excruciatingly lonely death, Jesus longed to see His followers love each other in God-revealing community with the same love that, with one three-hour lapse, eternally flows back and forth between the Father and the Son and the Holy Spirit.

I have a long way to go in becoming a clear answer to that prayer. I imagine you do too. But go there we must, if we want to be His disciples. *Relational sin* burdened Jesus the most. It ruins community. *Relational holiness* excited Him the most. It restores community among us in a way that resembles the eternal community of God. It brings heaven's *relational* kingdom to earth among His disciples, which then serves as the platform from which to make the world a better place.

Renounce all that you have. That is the third cost to count in order to become disciples. As long as we claim our primary citizenship to be in this world, as long as we care more about our life *here* than our life *there*, we will claim ownership of everything we have that improves our quality of life, and if we're socially sensitive we will provide others with whatever we can give them that will improve their quality of life.

Priorities then become reversed. Bringing God's *relational* kingdom to earth by becoming increasingly *relationally* holy—by Christians learning to put Christ's way of relating on display first to each other and then overflowing with Jesus-like love to the world—takes a backseat in favor of devoting our first efforts to making this world a better place to live. The quality of our community becomes a secondary priority. And we then live outside of God's will, giving way to the third face of entitlement: *we all deserve a better life now.*

And then, whether consciously or unconsciously, we will adopt an attitude soiled with narcissism.

- Society (church, government, culture) exists to give me a good life.
- Those with resources—the wealthy, the talented, the entrepreneurs—are morally obligated to cooperate with my desire to get what I deserve.
- Something is enormously wrong with a world that doesn't provide what everyone needs to enjoy life. Nothing matters more than fixing that problem. No need to wait for Jesus to return and make all things new. Let's do it now.

Jesus speaks into this attitude. In no uncertain terms, He insists we lay no claim to having what we want from this world. That is the third of the three costs of discipleship. We count it, we renounce all that we have, and we respond to life's difficulties, deprivations, and disappointments with confidence that a good story is now unfolding, with resolute hope for a better day yet to come, an eternal day as citizens of heaven's kingdom.

Jesus calls us to count the cost of discipleship before resolving to follow Him on the narrow road, acknowledging that we must:

- *depend* on no one but Him to provide both the desire and power to live the abundant life of loving like Jesus.
- never *demand* the experience of complete satisfaction but rather gratefully anticipate complete and always deepening satisfaction in the next life.
- humbly, without a false posture of self-deprecation, accept that we *deserve* nothing good and instead trust that, thanks to God's grace, everything good is on its way (such trust requires, of course, that we accurately understand what defines *good*).

As strangers and pilgrims in this world on a mission for God, to put Jesus on display, we *are* entitled to all the privileges of citizenship in heaven, privileges that for now center in bringing the relational kingdom of the Trinity into our relationships by pouring divine love from our new hearts into the hungry hearts of everyone to whom we are called.

Remember this as we now move on to part 2: the question to ask is *not* how well we are depending on Jesus alone, demanding nothing for ourselves, and accepting that we deserve nothing good. None of us will do especially well in measuring up to these impossible-sounding standards until we see the face of Jesus, literally. Only then will the three faces of entitlement be forever blotted out.

We must rather ask how passionately we long to count each cost. It is our *thirst* to live well that frees us to walk the narrow road, not our *success* in living well. It is the thirsty, not the falsely and prematurely satisfied, whom Jesus welcomes as disciples. When we're on the narrow road, both our longing and our ability to tell God's good story by how we relate slowly deepens, and we spiritually form—never fully till heaven but substantially in this life.

Pause for a moment. Where are you now? Are you aware that there is a better love, a love that when poured into another generates a different kind of happiness, a better way to relate that puts the love of Jesus on display? Can you see that, like everybody else, including me, you fall short of the relational glory of God?

If so, I hope you feel no pressure to love better but rather only desire, with a yearning that rises up from who you truly are, to be a person designed to know the happiness of knowing God well by revealing Him to others by how you relate.

The Trinity is telling the story of His love. What must we know in order to tell that story by how we live?

THE GOOD NEWS THAT ONLY DISCIPLES KNOW IS GOOD

Tired? Burned out on religion? Too much pain? Too many disappointments?

All of the above.

Come home to Me. I'll show you how to love like Me, to be happy like Me.

How will I get there?

On a rough road.

Is there another path?

No.

Then show me the way!

Since you're now reading these words, I will assume you have worked your way through part 1. Before we move on to part 2, it might prove helpful for us to reflect a bit on what was presented in the first ten chapters. What I plan to offer in the following chapters will, I think, be more profitably understood if the ideas suggested thus far have found their way into both our minds and hearts. Think with me now as I remember and ponder the key ideas of part 1.

- Joy, what I call first thing happiness, is less a pleasant feeling in our stomachs and more a living reality in our souls that sustains us on the narrow road—a different kind of happiness.

  Question: Is this understanding of joy something we want more than second thing happiness, the pleasurable emotions we feel when the blessings we pray for come our way?

- Joy, the happiness Jesus knew even as He hung on the cross, can be recognizably alive in our souls in the worst of circumstances and during our experience of terrible emotional pain. Genuine joy will live in us with sustaining power only when we draw on the Spirit's passion and power in order to love God, to value relationship with Him as our greatest good, and to esteem sacrificing ourselves for the well-being of others as our greatest purpose.

  Question: Do we really believe that loving God and loving others is not only the greatest commandment but also is the sure and only route to the happiness we were created to know?

- Second thing prayers, prayers for blessings we unselfishly desire to enjoy and for healing we understandably long to experience, are *conditional* prayers: "Father, if it be Your will, if granting these requests will further and not hinder the Spirit's forming work in me, I fervently ask You to grant these petitions. If answers to these prayers will slow down or get in the way of my transformation in becoming a little Christ, I willingly surrender to Your good purpose."

  Question: Do we even want to keep second things in second place, knowing that they do generate the pleasant experience of second thing happiness? Are we in touch with a deeper desire for our greatest good, for the first thing of being relationally formed to increasingly resemble Jesus?

- First thing prayer is the prayer God promises to answer: "Whatever the cost, *make me a little Christ*. Father, may Your Spirit open the eyes of my heart to see Your beauty so that I'm left with no greater desire while I live in this world than to reveal Your Son's love to others by how I relate." The good work of forming Christ in us will continue "until it is finally finished on the day when Jesus Christ returns" (Phil. 1:6). That's a guarantee, straight from God.

  Question: With the psalmist, can we truthfully say, "I desire you more than anything on earth" (Ps. 73:25)? Are we in touch with the inconsolable longing in every soul, the desire for a satisfaction nothing in this world can provide, that cries out in joyful hope, "As the deer longs for streams of water, so I long for you, O God. I thirst for God, the living God. When can I go and stand before him" (42:1–2)?

  Do we most passionately pray most often for second things? Or with David, can we say without reserve, "One thing have I asked of the LORD, that will I seek after: that I may dwell in the house of the LORD all the days of my life, to gaze upon the beauty of the LORD and to inquire in his temple" (27:4 ESV)?

- No one can claim to be a true disciple of Jesus who has not counted the cost of following Him on the narrow road through life to *life*—through life in this world, with all its ups and downs, to the divine *life* of loving like Jesus. True disciples *depend* only on Jesus for all they need to love like Jesus. True disciples *demand* no satisfaction from this world but rather groan inwardly for the Spirit's transforming work as they wait eagerly for that work to be finally finished. True disciples confess they *deserve* nothing good but gratefully trust that God is working through all things to provide them with every good thing.

  Question: Are we merely self-centered fans of Jesus who assume He will provide us now with whatever we think is good? Or, as true disciples, do we hate our sin more than our pain? Do we loathe the self-centered passions still within us that corrupt our efforts to love like Jesus? And do we value God's forgiveness and the power His Spirit provides to grow in our likeness to Jesus more than we value the blessings of life?

As I ask myself these piercing questions, I become more aware that, like you, I am a double being. But no Christian is the double being described by Robert Louis Stevenson, a decent Dr. Jekyll who can find no joy in living decently and a Mr. Hyde who feels alive only when he indulges his shameful desires.

No, we are people who bear the image of the relational God of love, made alive in Christ and able to know joy as we love the way He loves us. But the tendency remains to value the immediate pleasures of sin, especially the pleasures of relational sin, more than we value the joy of suffering, sacrificial love.

The battle is on between the Spirit-planted desire to delight God by loving like His Son and the still inextinguishable demanding spirit in each of us that feels entitled to self-arranged protection from hurt and to self-satisfying available pleasures. It is the battle that is fought on the narrow road, the battle for a better love.

The Narrow Road Battle

The Holy Trinity—Father, Son, and Holy Spirit—on one side calling us into their relational dance of love.

The unholy trinity—the world, the flesh, and the devil—on the other side seducing us to live for self-protection and self-enhancement.

In our redeemed spirit that is alive to God, we are drawn to the divine dance. In our flesh still beguiled by Satan, the invitation to look after ourselves feels like an invitation to life. The battle is on, but truth will set us free to remain on the narrow road to real life. Part 2 sets out the truth that frees us to respond to the Holy Trinity and to resist the unholy trinity, to realize what it means to discover joy in relational holiness, to battle for a better love.

It's time now to hear the tale of two stories, the story of God that leads us through struggle to *life*, and the story of Satan that leads us through love-denying pleasure to death.

11

A Tale of Two Stories

Just as God has communicated many truths to man, so has Satan endeavored to bring in many errors . . . he operates as one wearing the very face of truth.

Samuel Bolton[1]

Beneath the surface of everything we see, two stories are being told, one by God and another by Satan. Correction: only Satan's story lies hidden *beneath* what is visible. God's story, the true and therefore good one, is in every moment unfolding *around* us and *in* us, *above* and *beneath* where we live and all that's happening to us. It's a story unseen by most but always seeable through the lens of Scripture and on dazzling display to everyone who battles for love, to everyone who realizes that learning to love really is a battle, a battle to tell God's story by how we relate.

As we now begin to explore the good news revealed in God's story, news that only disciples who are counting the cost of following Jesus on the narrow road will recognize as incomparably good, it will be helpful to keep three things in mind.

First, *only as we walk the narrow road will our eyes slowly open to see the story God is telling.* You can know God's story is coming into view when what you see evokes wonder, some fear, and even a little obstinacy. The narrowing of the narrow road becomes felt when we sense our reflexive resistance to the life God makes available to His disciples, and when we become aware that a story opposing God's seems attractive.

That opposing story, authored by Satan, offers what appears to be sensible advice: protect yourself from hurt in your relationships. Don't risk being seen and unwanted. Hide! Cry injustice when you're treated poorly and dwell on the pain caused by the offender's wrongdoing. When you see wrong in yourself, explain it as the product of how you've been wronged. Forgive your offender if you must, but only as a means to persuade the cad to treat you better. Avoid true forgiveness. It only opens you to more hurt. Satan's counsel makes sense—if your goal is to look out for yourself, for your felt well-being on your terms and on your timetable.

But the appeal of God's story, though naturally resisted, reaches deeper. From somewhere that I vaguely realize defines who I truly am, I feel strangely drawn to a different way to relate, a risky way, the self-sacrificing kind of love revealed in God's story. The danger is clear: God suffers because He loves. I realize that if I love like God I'll suffer like God, never as intensely but still painfully. And yet a desire to love like Jesus rises up from the dry ground in my heart, like a trickle of cool water bubbling up from an unseen spring in the desert.

Two stories are told, each in its own way enticing. Which one will I choose? A "double being" tension is felt, and I realize I'm on the narrow road, assuming I'm counting the cost of discipleship.

Second (and an uncomfortable thought), *we do not need to see Satan's story in order to follow its script.* Relating like the devil comes naturally and it feels right. With effortless ease we attribute responsibility for our broken (or breaking) relationships to another. "I'm not perfect," we glibly confess, "but someone needs to realize how badly I've been treated."

Remaining blind to Satan's story works to hell's advantage. When we don't realize whose idea it is that we relate as we do, we fail to recognize and blush over the evil we are releasing into others. We see little need for severe repentance. Token apologies will do. Just keep the devil out of it, we say, not realizing that's a sure way to keep him in.

Third, *we do need to see God's story most fully made known in the life and death of Jesus in order to engage in the battle for a better love.* You can know you have glimpsed the truest love story ever told when you are awed by what you see. Nothing compares with the relational beauty of the divine community, a beauty put on display for us to see how God relates to the self-centered rebels we've all become.

Only when we are stunned by the relational beauty of the Trinity will we become aware of the evil energizing how we relate—hiding, defending, protecting, demanding. And only then will we humbly admit that supernatural resources are needed for divine love to flow out of us into others. It's undeniable—better love courts danger. It opens us to pain. Distorted love (which isn't love at all) is safer. It recommends that we keep our guard up.

Let me sum up those three thoughts in two sentences. First, the more clearly we see both stories, the more resolutely, freely, and passionately we will remain on the narrow road in the battle for a better love. Second, the tale of two stories must be told.

Satan's Evil Tale

Beneath everything—the movies we watch, the sermons we hear, the health concerns we face, the friendships we pursue, the marriages we struggle with—Satan is messing with us. He is always whispering a very bad story into our minds and hearts. The story he tells is disguised to look good and to serve our interests, but it never does. And yet because he stays hidden as the teller of the tale, because we don't recognize that the story we find appealing is evil, we like what we hear and see nothing wrong with our attraction to what we fail to realize is evil. Following its relational script feels reflexive, not chosen. It's how we naturally relate from birth. Through advertisements, celebrities, politicians, and sometimes pastors, Satan encourages us to look out for ourselves. And without thinking, we respond, "Of course! Isn't that the best way to live?"

The deception began in Eden. The serpent persuaded Eve to believe a disastrous lie, that the happiness God created her to enjoy could not be found in God, specifically not in the way He arranged things. A forbidden tree indeed. It seemed clear that God was holding back from Eve what she could most enjoy. And she was supposed to call Him good? Given her deception, she quite sensibly took matters into her own hands, feeling fully justified in arranging for the happiness she wanted.

Adam, however, was not deceived (see 1 Tim. 2:14). And that made his choice to eat the forbidden fruit all the more culpable. He did not question the adequacy of God's provision. But he did wonder about the sufficiency of God's love. Let me explain.

Unlike Eve, Adam knew that nothing *outside God's generous provision* would deliver the deep happiness they both longed to experience. But he was not certain that the resources *inside God's loving heart* would prove enough to overcome evil with good. Up to this point in his life, Adam could only see God's lavish blessings. He knew God was generous. But was He forgiving?

Satan seized his opening. The depths of God's merciful and gracious love were not yet visible to Adam but were in danger of becoming visible now that Eve's sin had created the opportunity for their display. Might Eve die then resurrect? Satan didn't want to take that chance.

With the anti-God virus now in her spiritual bloodstream, Eve offered forbidden fruit to Adam. I suspect Satan put it in Adam's mind to realize what a good thing he had going with Eve. He didn't want to lose it. So, without faith that something wonderful lay deep in God's heart that could be revealed in response to Eve's sin, Adam made a fateful decision that set every one of his descendants on a broad road. He turned away from the God he knew and joined his wife in mutual rebellion. How else could he be with her? What would life be like without her? It was a bad decision. But like every sin, it seemed good in the moment.

Satan's story continues to be told. To this day, it shapes the way every one of us naturally thinks in at least two ill-fated ways. First, with our now self-determined understanding of what is good and what is evil, we doubt whether the better love of Jesus will in fact birth the happiness of Jesus. We wonder if there even is such a thing. Second thing happiness, we know, is available. Better to aim for the satisfying emotions that come when others treat us well and when life goes our way. Like Eve, we let hell's wisdom direct us to look out for ourselves, chasing after whatever happiness we can find in this world, protecting ourselves as best we can from relational hurt, and resigning ourselves to whatever troubles we must bear.

Second, we may give tacit assent to the belief that battling for a better love is "the Christian thing to do" and that it might pay off with some semblance of joy, but we're afraid the battle's cost will be too painful. Suppose we stop protecting ourselves from relational hurt. Do we then just "live hurt" rather than "live loved"? What if we do ask forgiveness for our "minimal" contribution to a broken relationship when the other person's contribution feels so much greater? Will that make us feel better? Does Jesus really want us to give our best to people who give us their worst? That is what He did.

Like Adam, we remain unconvinced that the beauty of loving like Jesus will bring anything beautiful into our lives. Will God provide the happiness we long to know? We're not sure.

God's Beautiful Tale

The holy story told by the Holy One is about holy love, what I like to call *relational holiness*, an "other" kind of love that without the example of Jesus we wouldn't believe could even exist in real life. Only in God's story as told by Jesus do we see two unimaginable relational passions played out: *mercy*, not receiving from God what we deserve, and *grace*, receiving from God what we don't deserve—both made available to us at an incalculable cost paid entirely by God.

Is it possible to relate to others in like manner, to love others as Jesus loved us? Are we to *not* give others what they deserve: criticism, a cold shoulder, payback? And are we to give others what they *don't* deserve: forgiveness, kindness, love? Not until our sin against God reduces us to consuming gratitude for His mercy and grace will we even entertain the possibility of offering mercy and grace to someone who has hurt us.

Paul told us to "fix our gaze on things that cannot be seen" (2 Cor. 4:18). Is he telling us to do what no one can do, to see what is unseeable? Or is he saying that eyes opened by God's Spirit can see what otherwise cannot be seen, a love story that must be seen, God's story, if we're to enter the battle to display His kind of love?

I believe the latter. But questions remain: What good story is God telling and wants to tell through you when romantic passion for your spouse has died, when you discover your fourteen-year-old son is smoking pot, when your close friend turns on you for no reason you're aware of, when your adult daughter tries to take her own life? What good story was God telling me when the doctor told me my cancer was back?

Let's come at the questions from another angle: When a doctor successfully treats liver cancer with a painless, noninvasive procedure (which, thank God, is my recent experience), does the good in God's story involve *more* than the warmly welcomed medical outcome? Is the same story told in good times and bad, in your satisfying relationships and in your difficult ones? Is the same good story told when you drive to the hospital for surgery or to the golf course for a fun outing with friends? If so, *what is it?*

That question has an answer. But the answer will not grip us with a sense of delighted privilege unless we are disciples following Jesus on the narrow road. To folks on the broad road, the answer will sound merely religious, something to think about on Sunday that proves itself useless during the week. And don't forget this: no one is on the narrow road who has not counted the cost of becoming a disciple of Jesus. Look again at the three-part cost Jesus told us to count.

Cost 1: we must agree with Jesus that only He can provide joy, the happiness we were created to enjoy; and, as a result, we accept that we're entitled to nothing from anyone.

Cost 2: we must be prepared to deny our naturally compelling desire to draw life from others and to carry the cross of unrequited love, to continue loving those who hurt us.

Cost 3: we must declare, God helping us, that we are willing to relinquish all sense of entitlement to depending for our well-being on whatever happiness is available in this world.

As I remind myself of those three costs, I'm surprised that even a few sign up to follow Jesus as disciples on the narrow road. If I fail to see the story of God unfolding in my life and if I fail to believe that God's story leads to the happiness He created me to enjoy, I realize that I will not be one of the few. God help me. I want to be!

God's Story Revealed in the Answers to Seven Questions

Some years ago, something obvious dawned on me: *God did not write the Bible to answer all the questions that everyday life drives me to ask.* Should I confront this person or back off? What treatment facility is best for a friend's daughter who is addicted to heroin? If

I don't take this job, will a better one come along? The questions are endless. The answers are rarely clear. I must not expect to find a Bible verse that tells me exactly what to do as I face life's challenges or, if I handle trials well, what blessings will follow.

God wrote the Bible, I now believe, to answer the questions I need to ask in order that I may know God and make Him known to others by how I relate, and in so doing, know the happiness of Jesus. As that truth took hold in my thinking and affected how I read the Bible, I began to see seven questions that God has answered in the sixty-six love letters He's written to us. I call them the Seven Questions of Spiritual Theology, and that term requires brief explanation.

Biblical theology, a term familiar to seminary students, articulates truth that emerges from and can be defended by biblical study. Systematic theology, another term that describes the content of many seminary courses, arranges biblically supported truths into a system of knowledge that can be organized in a doctrinal statement and unpacked in thick textbooks.

Spiritual theology, as I define the term, weaves biblical theology and systematic theology together to tell a story, God's story of love from eternity past to eternity future. And His story speaks directly into ours, revealing how the little story of our lives can tell the grand story of God if we let our understanding of that story shape *how we relate*. Spiritual theology stirs up the relational life of Jesus in those who are drawn to the story it tells. Perhaps spiritual theology as I understand it could better be referred to as *relational* theology. But for now, we'll stick with the first term.

In the remaining chapters, as best and as simply as I can, I suggest answers to the Seven Questions of Spiritual Theology that together tell God's story. I also suggest Satan's wrong answers to each question that he would have us believe, answers that together tell his evil story. As we see those two stories, we feel a tension arising from the attraction we feel to the prospect of telling each one. It is then that a life of crucial choices begins and we find ourselves living life on the narrow road, battling for a better love, to know the desire and the power and the wisdom to love like Jesus.

The Seven Questions of Spiritual Theology

1. Who is God?
2. What is He up to?
3. Who are we?
4. What's gone wrong?
5. What has God done about our problem?
6. How is the Spirit working to implement the divine solution to our human problem?
7. How can we cooperate with the Spirit's work?

12

True or False?

It's Sometimes Hard to Tell

A story is precisely the sort of thing that cannot be understood until you have heard the whole of it.

C. S. Lewis[1]

In all of history, only two cosmic stories have been told and continue to be told. Tell one by how you live, especially by how you relate, and you will become a little Christ—slowly, with many setbacks, but it will happen. And you will know joy.

Tell the other and, more quickly because telling it comes more naturally, you will be twisted into a little devil. You can come across to others as nice, friendly, concerned, and helpful, believe you embrace each of those virtues, and still be mostly committed to your own well-being. The devil has many of us fooled. Self-centeredness is easily hidden beneath congeniality and, even when recognized, is often seen as necessary to personal comfort and therefore not really wrong.

"Loving" like the devil keeps us safe from the dangers of loving like Jesus. It also keeps us safe from knowing love's joy. A heart never given away for the sake of another cannot be broken—hurt, yes, but not broken. A self-protected heart (to be distinguished from an appropriately and biblically guarded heart) hardens over time and becomes incapable of love, shielded by an impermeable crust from both the suffering of Jesus and His happiness.

Only Christlikeness, the certain result of telling God's story, displays a willing vulnerability to relational heartbreak, but never to heartbreak without hope. Relating like Jesus opens your eyes to catch glimpses of the kind of beauty that all of us were created to enjoy, *relational* beauty, the beauty of love freely given to another at any cost to self, the beauty fully displayed only in Jesus.

It is dangerously possible to think we're loving like Jesus when we're relating like Satan. It happens in Christian marriages, in apparently close friendships, and in good churches. Little matters more than knowing whose story we're telling as we relate with family and friends. Knowing whose story we're telling releases us either to gratefully worship or to purposefully repent. Only one story is true and good. The other one is false and evil.

The Seven Questions of Spiritual Theology call for answers that when woven together tell a story, a story in which all other stories become chapters. God tells His story by answering the seven questions in the Bible. Satan pushes his answers through a culture that glorifies self—how is life going for *me!*—and his answers appeal to our bent toward self-protection. But he's tricky, a master of deception. He cleverly crafts his answers to sound as if they come from God. As a result, thirsty people drink cool water laced with tasteless poison.

I offer what I understand to be God's answers, revealed in the Bible, to each of the seven questions. And I suggest how the angel of light, the father of lies, provides answers that can appear to be good theology, answers that tell a story with a plot that seems to serve our best interests. But keep this in mind: *God's answers can be trusted even when they don't feel persuasive. Satan's answers are designed to feel persuasive but they can never be trusted.* May God help us to recognize which story we're telling by how we relate.

Remember the C. S. Lewis quote that headlined this brief chapter: "A story is precisely the sort of thing that cannot be understood until you have heard the whole of it." The whole of the story we need to hear begins in eternity past and continues into eternity future. Seven chapters unfold the drama. Let's now look at each one.

13

Question 1

Who Is God?

> Though many beings are called gods by men, there is only one living and true God, and He is radically different from anything in creation. . . . And, quite importantly, we cannot know other things rightly without knowing God rightly.
>
> John Frame[1]

Theology professor John Frame opens his 437-page book propounding what it means to have the knowledge of God with five short sentences: "What is the 'object' of the knowledge of God? In knowing God, what do we know? Well, God, of course! So what remains to be said? Much."[2]

And I would add, much that's wrong! (Not from Frame, however. His book is exceptional.)

Here's the problem: I'm hearing voices. No, I'm not psychotic. I'm on the narrow road, and that's where followers of Jesus hear two voices—God's, of course, but Satan's too. Sincere Christians move on this road toward putting Jesus on display by relating with a better love, so it's no surprise that the devil has no intention of leaving true disciples alone. He wants no one to see Jesus. They might like Him.

Bear with a seemingly trivial personal story that illustrates the struggle created by hearing these two voices.

Patience is not on my short list of noticeable virtues. And punctuality has not made its way onto the much longer list of my wife's laudable strengths. The collision is inevitable. It's happened many times.

"Honey, are you ready?" I ask. "If we're going to get there on time, we need to leave right now."

"I'm ready," she answers. "Back the car out of the garage. I'll be there in a minute."

To God, a day is no different than a thousand years. To Rachael, a minute means an indeterminate time.

Ten minutes later, I'm sitting in our car, out of the garage, engine running, and I'm thumping the steering wheel wondering *What on earth could she be doing?*

Three minutes more and she finally arrives, opening the passenger door, smiling, and saying, "We can go now." Two voices speak from within me, audible only to my internal ears. One is heard with stronger passion.

I have every right to ask her what kept her so long. She's always late. I deserve an explanation. She needs to own up to her habit of never *being ready on time. I'm really ticked.*

As words energized by impatience form on my tongue, a second voice speaks. Perhaps maturity yet to come will someday let me hear it first.

I love this woman. She is late rather often and I really do wish she were on time. But Jesus accepts me with far greater faults. I can ask what kept her, I suppose. But I'm less interested in her answer, and even in her being ready when she says she is, and more interested in her knowing that her lateness will never diminish my love for her one bit.

Two voices, one directing me toward a comment that would feel satisfying to me but at her expense; the other that would allay any fear in her that my love is conditional on her meeting my expectations.

As she fastens her seat belt, I'm walking on the narrow road. Two voices. Two possible responses to my wife. One satisfies my flesh. The other blesses her soul. The battle is on.

I want to know who God is, to know Him so well that I enjoy Him as I enjoy no one else, and more than anything, I want to know Him in a way that draws me to cooperate with His purposes in me and through me. But—think back to my earlier discussion of Dr. Jekyll and Mr. Hyde—I remain a double being. I'd strongly prefer to hear only God's voice, but with my ever-present inclination to honor self-interest above God's glory, I hear Satan's as well and, worse, I can be drawn to what he says. Sometimes I'm not entirely certain whose voice I'm hearing. The devil is tricky. Like the Israelites in Isaiah's day, I can be maneuvered into calling evil good and good evil (see Isa. 5:20). Insisting on fair, sensitive treatment from others seems good. The demand is evil.

I remember what Jesus said, that His sheep "know his voice" (John 10:4 ESV), but I remember, too, that Paul warned us that false teachers would gain a hearing in churches, disguising themselves as "apostles of Christ," and even Satan, Paul adds, "disguises himself as an angel of light" (2 Cor. 11:13–14). Knowing when we're hearing God's voice and discerning when Satan is speaking as if he were God is not always easy.

Who is God? Two opposing voices answer this question. Could the devil disguise his voice so well that followers of Jesus might think we're listening to God when Satan speaks? Of course. It happens more often than we know. But discernment, which includes the sensitivity to recognize who is answering the first question of spiritual theology (and the other six as well), deepens the longer we keep walking on the narrow road.

I hope this book encourages you to begin your journey on the always narrowing road to life—for some, perhaps for the first time. For others, it may be beginning again, getting back on the narrow road after a disillusioning time in the prodigal's pigpen. I count myself among these "others."

I've heard the voice of Jesus. Every Christian has or they wouldn't be a Christian. I've known what it means to feel close to God, to love Jesus, to recognize the Spirit's nudging. But now, as I write this chapter, I'm aware that a thin crust has slowly been forming over my heart, weakening my appetite to know God and make Him known. Expressing irritability toward my wife can seem justified and strangely satisfying. I think I've taken a break from the battle for a better love. Something vile and stubbornly deep within me wants to keep God *as I know Him* at a distance. Could it be that I've been listening to the devil telling me who God is?

For me, asking this first question is no academic exercise. I long to know God, not merely to know about Him but to know Him in the beauty of how the three divine Persons relate, and how God relates with me and with everyone in this apparently God-forsaken world. But I'll never see the beauty that compels worship, that draws obedience, and that forms relational Christlikeness if I mistake Satan's answers for God's.

The devil knows the Bible. He knows how to twist truth into true-sounding lies that serve his purposes. Among others, Satan offers two understandings of who God is that can deceive unsuspecting and therefore unguarded Christians. Satan's first answer: *God is almighty.* Of course that is true. And the devil knows it. God created everything, is ruler over everything, is sovereign in everything, and is the final judge of everyone. He has the power to do whatever He wants to do. And He has made it clear that He is holy and will reward obedience and punish disobedience. He says so directly in Deuteronomy 28:1–6, 15–19. I want to know God to love Him. Satan knows God and hates Him. So he emphasizes and calls spotlight attention to God's power, dismissing His grace as secondary. That emphasis, if not seen as the prelude to further revelation of God's character in Jesus, reduces God to Islam's Allah, centrally known as the all-powerful one.

In my early days as a Christian, God's love and grace seemed a mere backdrop to His severity. In school, on days when a big test was scheduled, I rarely missed my required time with God. I had no desire to draw close to God; I simply wanted to get this divine, demanding, all-powerful policeman off my back and get on his good side by breaking no laws.

Even now, so many years later, residual superstition remains. I can feel the urge to be especially law-abiding before I preach a sermon or lead a seminar or write a book, or when I welcome Rachael into the car. Under Satan's unrecognized tutelage, thinking I'm being wisely accountable to God, my choice to not indulge a favorite sin can become a manipulative technique to earn from God what I most want, which, given that motive, certainly is not Him. A patient response to Rachael could be designed to shame her into becoming more punctual rather than to encourage her with evidence of unconditional love.

What Satan says is not always the problem. More often, it's what he leaves out. God is almighty but there's more to be said. Much more. Paul passes on what he has heard from the Sovereign Judge: "The law was designed to last only until the coming of the child who was promised" (Gal. 3:19). And now that Jesus has come, we have been "made right with God . . . through faith in Christ Jesus" (vv. 24, 26). The Judge is now smiling. We're invited to party in His chambers.

Satan's half-truth, his evil specialty, leaves us feeling pressure to do what we can't, to be who we aren't. Consider the result of seeing

God as primarily power, as an unfeeling judge. Either *despair* overwhelms us (I can't measure up) or blind, foolish *pride* exalts us (I do measure up).

An angry wife confronts her husband: "You really hurt me. I don't know if I can ever forgive you."

How might her husband respond if he understands God to be only a powerful enforcer of the law?

The Way of Despair

To himself: *What am I supposed to do? I never do anything right.*

To her: "I know I really blew it. I'm sorry. I don't know why I always mess up so badly."

The Way of Pride

To himself: *Where does she get off being so mad? I've put up with worse from her.*

To her: "Look, you've done nothing but criticize me. And I've been pretty patient with you. Give me a break."

But Satan has another biblical-sounding answer to question 1, this one better suited to today's sin-denying culture. "Evil" is now limited to heinous deeds such as murder, rape, and genocide and to social injustices like racist comments, moralistic bigotry, government corruption, and corporate greed. By those moral standards, I'm a rather good person. *Of course God loves me. Why wouldn't He?*

Today's culture, including our church culture, has little awareness of relational sin, of what it means to fall short of the relational glory of our Trinitarian God. To people who are wrongly content with congenial relating that leaves self-protective relating in place and requires little self-sacrifice, Satan explains who God is with another half-truth, this one more poorly defined.

Satan's second answer: *God is love.* Too often we reply, "Of course!" And we hear that profound truth to mean that *God is nice.*

Yes, Jesus died for us, and that was more than nice; that was extraordinary, self-sacrifice in the extreme. But now, as a result of Christ's atoning work on Calvary, God is no longer our judge and we're no longer criminals. It's true. We are forgiven and accepted, acquitted of all charges. Of course we're still not perfect, but whatever "little" we still do that is wrong is met with amazing grace. So—and here is where Satan deceives us—there really is no need to worry about the subtleties of relational sin, no need to discern where we fail to put the relational glory of Jesus on display, no need to battle for a better love. We're loving quite well, and our occasional shortcomings are understandable. God should be nice to us. So should everyone else. If God won't judge us, no one else should either.

Paul exposes the lie hidden in Satan's answer. Yes, Paul emphatically agrees, God is love, and our sin provides God the opportunity to showcase His love. But that truth raises a question: "Well then, should we keep on sinning so that God can show us more and more of his wonderful grace?" (Rom. 6:1). Paul answers with equal emphasis, "Of course not!" (v. 2). God's grace was never intended to encourage a casual attitude toward relational sin. The gospel means forgiveness *and relational formation*, learning to love like Jesus.

But Satan's reply to the same question is "Why not?" He wants us to think more about God's love and almost never about our sin. Why obsess about the barely recognizable self-centeredness that motivates our kindness to others? Why worry whether our friendly, outgoing personality charms others but fails to pour divine love into their empty souls? *Look, others fail me more than I fail them. I've got to take care of myself. God understands. He's nice. He wants me to feel good about myself.*

If Satan's first answer, "God is almighty," leads unwary Christians onto the broad road of despair or pride, his second answer, an intentionally misconstrued declaration that "God is love," leads us onto the broad road of entitlement, a warranted expectation that a loving God will give us the good life we want, or of greed, justified indulgence in providing ourselves with whatever pleasure we desire and protecting ourselves from whatever pain we fear. *God loves me. Of course He'll give me what I want. And He won't mind if I don't relate exactly like Jesus. I love others, and God, quite well. He wants me to feel good about myself. He loves me.*

An angry wife confronts her husband: "You really hurt me. I don't know if I can ever forgive you."

How might her husband respond if he understands God to be pleasantly nice?

The Way of Entitlement

To himself: *She makes a big deal out of everything. Why can't we just get along?*

To her: "I know I hurt you. I want to make it up to you. How about dinner tonight; maybe we can catch a movie?"

The Way of Greed

To himself: *She sees me as a loser. I might as well get a beer and look at porn.*

To her: "Since you can't accept me as I am, I see no point in talking about how to make things better."

Think back to Frame's comment that opened this chapter: "In knowing God, what do we know? Well, God, of course! So what remains to be said? Much." And, I added, *much that's wrong.*

But there is *so much that's right.* And everything about God that is radically different from everything in creation and from every created person, everything that is wonderful about God and everything that is true, flows from one soul-stirring but too glibly acknowledged center.

Who is God? God's answer: *God is relational.* Yes, He is almighty and He is love, and much more. But every expression of His power is energized by love. And His love is holy love, a commitment to the well-being of others at any cost to Himself, a commitment to what alone will bring well-being to others. And that is the ability to move into relationships with a better love, loving like Jesus that generates the happiness of Jesus. He wants to make us perfect in how we love. And He means to see that it happens. *So who is He?*

God is a three-Person community, one God who exists eternally as three fully divine but unique Persons, each fully disposed by His divine nature to relate selflessly, sacrificially, fully committed to the happiness of others. That way of relating is God's glory, God's *relational* glory, the glory that Jesus put on display and gave to us so we could enjoy the kind of community the Trinity eternally enjoys. Think of it: final reality in the universe is not a doctrinal statement that Christians affirm, it is a better love revealed in a divine community into which everyone is invited. True doctrine matters, for a thousand reasons, but none more important than that it reveals the better love that defines the Trinity.[3]

An angry wife confronts her husband. "You really hurt me. I don't know if I can ever forgive you."

How might her husband respond if he understands God to be a relational community of three divine Persons who love each other, and all people, with a better love?

To himself: *I can feel the urge to defend myself, criticize her, and back away, in order to feel better. My wife can be irritating, unfair, and late. But I really do want to put Jesus on display to her even when I think she's being unfair and unreasonable.*

To her: "I'm not sure how to move toward you right now. Are you willing to tell me what's happening in you as you think about how I've failed you? I want to respond to your hurt with what's best in me."

So now the story of the relational God begins. The next question follows: *What is He up to?* And I want to hear God's answer, not

149

Satan's. A lengthy quote from David Broughton Knox, a brilliant biblical scholar, will set the stage for our next chapter.

> Bestsellers today reflect the modern ideal of expressing yourself, of loving yourself, of liberating yourself from your relationships with other people, which constrict the development of your own personality. Through the revelation of the Trinity believers can see that this particular philosophical concept and social objective is contrary to reality and therefore will not bring the hoped-for benefits of happiness and peace. *A renewal of understanding of the Trinity and its implications for the way human life should be based will lead to the recognition that personal relationships which are other person–centered are ultimate in value for living, even though it should turn out that in serving those relationships it becomes impossible to pursue the chimera of gracious living, the balanced life and so-called authentic existence. Even life itself may be lost, but eternity will vindicate the reality of the basis of such actions.*[4]

That is a mouthful, a chewy feast. I'll do my best to deliver it in bite-sized portions.

14

Question 2

What Is God Up To?

He will make the feeblest and filthiest of us into a . . . dazzling, radiant, immortal creature, pulsating all through with such energy and joy and wisdom and love as we cannot now imagine. . . . The process will be long and in parts very hard; but that is what we are in for. Nothing less. He meant what He said.

C. S. Lewis[1]

The above quote comes close, I think, to what Lewis might have said had he been asked to answer question 2. As usual, his way of expressing himself is compellingly artistic. But am I among the feeblest and filthiest? Do I want to cooperate with a long and in parts painful process? Do these words stir excitement and hope? Or, even as I appreciate Lewis's writing talent, am I shrugging my shoulders in response to his thought, realizing that I'm interested in something other than becoming a "dazzling creature"? I might prefer a comfortable life.

If his words do tell us what God is up to, shouldn't they overwhelm us to the point of worship? But perhaps what he said erupted more from a great writer's imagination and a love for fantasy than from Scripture. We need to make sure we're hearing God answer the question. But what if God's answer provokes another hesitation, another shoulder shrug? Perhaps I prefer to believe that the Bible provides an answer that is quite different from Lewis's. Maybe something like this: "God will make every sincere and moral Christian into a happily blessed creature, pulsating with a zest for life that draws many to join in the excitement. The process may hit a few bumps, but a positive attitude (think of it as trusting God) will quickly provide abundant blessings to smooth the way. Heaven later; a good life now. What more could anyone ask? Praise God!"

The first answer, the one Lewis gave, informs us that God is up to making every Jesus follower into a certain kind of *person*. The second guarantees that God will provide us with a certain kind of *life*: good family, good friends, good health, good job, and the like—perhaps even a punctual wife.

Which answer to question 2 has more immediate appeal? Your twenty-three-year-old son has just been jailed for dealing drugs. Of course it breaks your heart. It breaks God's too. Do you most fervently pray for a better love, for the power to love your son well, in order to delight God and to reveal Jesus to your son? Or are you consumed with the intense desire that your son will find God in jail and turn his life around, so consumed with your son straightening out that nothing matters more? Shouldn't the latter reflect God's endgame?

In too many relational moments, especially those when I feel criticized or not taken into account, I want nothing more from God than His cooperation with my efforts to feel good about myself, to enjoy happiness as I want to experience it, to secure my entitled right to respectful treatment. In those moments, justice as I define it trumps love as God defines it. *Shouldn't* He cooperate? An injustice has brought pain into my life. Doesn't God hate injustice and love me? I want a life that is blessed, with all problems resolved. Is that so wrong?

Nowhere is Satan more cunningly tricky than when he answers question 2. If he has already convinced us (question 1) that God is either a rule-maker who rewards rule-keepers with the favor they want or a doting grandfather who has no greater pleasure than spoiling his still self-centered grandkids, then the soil of our minds has been plowed to receive the devil's soul-deadening answer to the second question as though it were life-giving seed.

In every person's life, times come when we must cry out, "God, what are You doing? Where are You? I want to trust You. I believe You're good. I know You love me. But my life is a disaster and I'm a mess. And You aren't helping at all. *God, what are You up to?*" Only an atheist's fatalism can suppress that question when life gets difficult.

I'm not an atheist. I'm not a fatalist. I believe that a personal, relational God of infinite power and wisdom and love exists, and in every moment of my life is carrying out what He knows is a good plan. I'm persuaded that everything that happens in me and to me and around me is a chapter, perhaps a very painful one, in a very good story. I believe in the mystery of providence. In the hard times, it is that belief, a belief I cannot shake, that explodes into the question: *God, what are You up to?*

You've read the first thirteen chapters of this book. You know what I understand to be God's answer to that question. There are several ways to put it. Here's one: God is right now devoting His unlimited resources of power and wisdom and love to forming those who receive the gospel into disciples who relate like Jesus. He has not promised to smooth out life's bumps with new or restored blessings. He is making us into people who radiate love, for three reasons: to delight the Trinity, to release the happiness of Jesus into His followers, and, through Christ-revealing disciples, to draw others into the Trinity's perfectly loving community. Every other good thing—enjoying life's blessings, promoting social justice, healing cancer, feeding the hungry, rescuing the politically oppressed, advancing medical science, campaigning for principled government, and everything else that's good, whether granted or denied—flows out of God's central agenda.

My answer is similar to Lewis's, though less eloquent. But does it square with God's? Six passages from the Bible will let us know.

1. "For God knew his people in advance, and he chose them *to become like his Son*" (Rom. 8:29). Worthy of worship like Jesus? Or relationally loving like Jesus?

2. "Oh, my dear children! I feel as if I'm going through labor pains for you again, and they will continue *until Christ is fully developed in your lives*" (Gal. 4:19). Fully equipped with sovereign power that once created and now upholds the universe? Or fully formed to relate with the better love of Jesus?

3. "Even before he made the world, God loved us and chose us in Christ *to be holy and without fault in his eyes*" (Eph. 1:4). Holy and without fault merely by external standards? Or relationally holy and without fault in the eyes of our relationally holy and faultless God?

4. "Through Christ . . . you were cleansed from your sins . . . so now you must . . . *love each other deeply with all your heart*" (1 Pet. 1:21–22). Are we to be satisfied with ourselves when we're nice to people, even kind? Or are we to be grateful for the privilege of sacrificing ourselves for others in ways that self-interest thinks foolish?

5. "Those who say they live in God should live their lives as Jesus did. . . . This old commandment—to love one another—is the same message you heard before. Yet it is also new. Jesus lived the

truth of this commandment, *and you also are living it*" (1 John 2:6–8). Am I? Are you? Are we in the battle for a better love?

6. Let's now hear directly from Jesus: "So now I am giving you a new commandment: Love each other. *Just as I have loved you, you should love each other. Your love for one another will prove to the world that you are my disciples*. . . .This is my command: Love each other" (John 13:34–35; 15:17). Prove to others that we belong to Jesus by making it our priority to change the world? Or by first loving within the community of faith with a better love and *then* as a loving community reaching out to the world?

The Scripture is clear. God *may* provide some or even most of the blessings we want and pray for. He *may* see to it that my cancer never returns. He *may* reach your son in jail with His forgiving and renewing grace. Pray for the blessings you desire. But count on the good that God is up to. He *will* make every cost-counting disciple into a little Christ, in growing measure during this life and in full measure in the next. He *will* put Jesus on display by how we Christians relate with a better love, if our deepest desire is to be relationally formed like Jesus. And it is. That desire is lodged securely and fully alive in the heart of every true Christian.

But here is where the battle is fought. Satan wants to keep us out of touch with our holy desire to love like Jesus and in touch only with our "second thing" desires. I know the devil's working when I feel my longing to be loved by family and friends more easily than I feel my longing to love them, when I feel my desire to be healed of the relational wounds I've suffered as stronger than I feel my desire to love others while unhealed wounds in me continue to cause pain, and when my wish to live emotionally energized as I face each day's opportunities and challenges feels more necessary to my well-being than discovering the power to love well when I'm exhausted and down.

He's shrewd. The devil wants us to fixate on two legitimate desires, the longing for *community* and for *healing*. He persuades us that God is up to nothing better than satisfying those two desires. Let me draw again from C. S. Lewis to make clear what I mean.

In *Mere Christianity*, Lewis suggests we get offtrack on our Christian journey by closely attending to two important matters and largely ignoring a more important third. He makes his point by envisioning several ships sailing in formation. Each pilot is properly concerned with avoiding a collision with the other ships and with seeing to it that the vessel is seaworthy, with an engine in good working order and a hull that doesn't leak. If a problem surfaces, the pilot dispatches technicians to fix what's wrong.

But suppose the pilots were not clearly settled on the fleet's intended direction. If that were so, they would have no way of knowing if they were on course. Then, as Lewis puts it, "However well the fleet sailed, its voyage would be a failure if it were meant to reach New York and actually arrived in Calcutta."[2]

His point is obvious and important. *We need to know where Jesus is taking us.* To what destination does the narrow road lead? Is it possible we believe He is up to one thing when in fact He is up to quite another? Have we lost our way without knowing it?

We are, of course, rightly concerned with getting along with each other and avoiding relational collisions. But to what end? For what purpose? Are we looking merely to enjoy community? Or are we more resolved to display Jesus by relating with a better love, even to those who bump into us, perhaps intentionally?

And thanks largely to our modern addiction to counseling, our culture, including our Christian culture, is obsessed with emotional healing. When we feel emotional pain, relief becomes our priority. We want to feel whole. Of course. We all do. But again, to what end? For what purpose?

For so many of us, feeling good about who we are, perhaps by discovering our identity in Christ, has become an end, no longer a means to an end. It matters more to feel whole than to reveal Jesus to others. If we seek counseling or spiritual direction to overcome whatever gets in the way of loving like Jesus, then well and good. *But the purpose of spiritual direction is relational formation.* It must not stop at experiencing the presence of God in a way that brings rest and peace to our souls. The presence of God frees us to bring His presence to others. And that brings glory to God by revealing the wonder of His love. That is the end, the goal. And the goal of Christian counseling, too, must be nothing less. Otherwise it is not *Christian* counseling.

Satan has tricked us into valuing two good things for two bad reasons. Listen to how he sometimes answers question 2: *God has made it possible for you to belong to a safe, accepting, and supportive community. Honor God by claiming what He has made possible. Settle for nothing less. If this requires you to retreat from unsafe people, do so. God wants you to enjoy the satisfaction you can only feel when others treat you as you want—and deserve—to be treated. That is what He is up to in your life.*

And He wants you to feel whole, as a loved, secure woman or as a respected, valuable man. Pursue counseling, receive spiritual direction, listen to sermons with one hope in mind: that you feel good about who you are. There is no greater good.

Satan is a liar and a clever one. *Of course* God is delighted when His children enjoy good community. "How good and pleasant it is when brothers dwell in unity" (Ps. 133:1 ESV). And He desires that our relational pain be relieved. "He heals the brokenhearted and binds up their wounds" (147:3 ESV). It is good in His eyes and in ours when ships sailing together don't collide but move in harmony with each other and when their internal workings function properly. But to what end? For what purpose?

Good community and gentle healing can encourage us to battle for a better love. Acceptance from others and life-giving words from others help us access our deepest desire, to cooperate with God in what He is up to. Let me put it this way: *God passionately longs for us to know Him so well and to love Him so deeply that we embrace no greater good than increasing His happiness by revealing Jesus to others by how we relate. That is what He is up to, making true disciples. Loving with a better love is the center of worship. Nothing brings God more glory.*

Question 2, properly answered, motivates us to enter the battle for a better love, to live on the narrow road where we hear both God's story and Satan's and discover that the appeal of Satan's self-serving story is slowly being squeezed out of us by the beauty of the Triune God and the story He is telling. It is the narrow road traveled by Christians who again and again count the cost of discipleship that exposes both Satan's lies and how easily we are drawn to them, then surfaces a deeper attraction to God's truth. *That doesn't happen on the broad road where we remain comfortable with our relational sin.* Only the narrow road leads us to where God is taking us, to become who, by God's grace, we are, who we were created to be, and who we most long to become: better lovers.

And that is what it means to be human, to love like Jesus and experience His happiness. Remember the fall was downward to living as subhumans. It's time to discover our capacity to live fully alive as human beings. And that brings us to the third question of spiritual theology: *Who are we?* Satan has an answer. We need to hear from God.

15

Question 3

Who Are We?

Oh souls created for greatness and summoned to it—*what are you doing?*

John of the Cross[1]

Let me offer a suggestion. Before reading this chapter, put the book down and for one minute reflect on this question: *Who am I?* Think beneath the obvious. You already know if you're a man or woman; married, single, or divorced; tall or short, overweight or thin, or just the right height and weight; employed or unemployed; a serious Christian, a casual Christian, or a non-Christian; perhaps an adherent of another religion or, as an elderly Jewish lady recently described herself to me, "a devout atheist."

Think beneath the obvious, the visible facts. *Who are you?* Ponder the question in perhaps a new way. Who do you understand yourself to be that influences the way you relate to people, the way you respond to life's happenings? A good friend hurts you. What does the way you deal with this friend reveal about who you are? A phone call brings difficult news. What does your emotional response to it tell you about yourself?

Think about it for one minute. I'm putting my pen down right now for sixty seconds to wonder about these same questions, questions that circle around question 3. *Who am I?*

There. It is now one minute later, actually closer to two.

I thought about yesterday's conversation with a good friend. I still feel a little miffed. I shared a trivial concern that I told him might indicate something more serious troubling me. I made it clear that I knew the surface concern was silly, worth only a brief chuckle and a comment such as, "Yeah, stupid little things sometimes bug me too." But he heard me say with some feeling that I suspected a bigger issue was rumbling beneath the inconsequential worry.

He replied, "Could be, I guess. But c'mon, sometimes I wonder if you think too much. Give yourself a break." He then changed the subject.

I felt dismissed, worthy of no curious interest. I could feel a sulk coming on. A counterdismissal came to mind, perhaps a pleasantly sarcastic, "Maybe you think too little." To myself, I said, *So much for him being a sensitive friend. Guess I'll do what I always do, just suck it up and play friendly. That's better than yelling at him, which I'd rather do. I feel failed, but I'm used to it. I'll do the Christian thing and overlook his hurtful comment.* (Note: thanks to being in the middle of writing this book, I did have a few better thoughts as well. But to make my point and to avoid sounding defensive, I'll not mention them.)

Now that I'm replaying that conversation in my mind, I wonder what a particular advice columnist would tell me if I wrote to her, described both what happened and how I felt, then asked what she thought would be a mature way to respond to my friend's disappointing comment. Suppose, too, I mentioned that I was a man of faith, a Christian. What counsel might she offer?

Here's my guess. I think it's a good one. I read her column in the newspaper every morning.

> You'll feel better about yourself if you share your feelings with your friend, but without coming across as judgmental or demanding. Letting him know how he impacted you would give him the chance to be a better friend. If he brushes you off, accept him for who he is, a good but imperfect friend, and move on.
>
> But don't move on by hiding yourself from others. Everyone needs someone to listen well to them and to be warmly curious about what they hear. Keep in mind that you often get what you give. Pay attention to how well you listen to others. You'll come across someone who will give you the attentive ear you need. Don't give up on people. You said you are a Christian. I believe in God too. You might want to ask Him to put you in touch with a better friend.

Notice what's obviously missing in that advice: *there is no thought given to what it would mean to offer a better love to a disappointing friend.* The counsel is aimed not toward my friend's well-being but rather toward my feeling better. With the happiness of Jesus? With His joy? Hardly.

The columnist is not directly concerned with helping me explore who I am, but her advice sends me in a certain direction. Who am I? She apparently thinks of me as a needy person, entitled to finding satisfaction from other people. And as someone with needs that must be met if I'm to feel good about myself, I should be encouraged to go on the lookout for someone—a new friend? a better spouse? a counselor I could pay to listen to me?—who will provide what I need.

Her understanding of how a Christian might respond to feeling hurt seems clear. I'm to trust God to lead me to a friend who will meet my needs. Again, no thought is given to what it would mean to put Jesus on display to people who cause me pain. I'm to use

God for my purposes, an invitation to narcissism. And a part of me responds warmly. *Good idea!*

Suppose I sought advice from John of the Cross. When I ponder the quote that headlined this chapter, I can imagine him weeping, experiencing the same emotion Jesus felt when He lamented over Jerusalem. "O Jerusalem, Jerusalem. . . . How often would I have gathered your children together as a hen gathers her brood under her wings, and you were not willing! . . . For I tell you, you will not see me again, until you say, 'Blessed is he who comes in the name of the Lord'" (Matt. 23:37–39 ESV).

In the Spirit of Jesus, perhaps John would ask me, "Oh, Larry, you who were created for greatness and summoned to it—*what are you doing*?" If I were to ask him what he meant, I think he might say, "You were created in the image of the God whose love pursues the unlovable. Greatness means to love like Jesus, the One who loved you when you dismissed Him, when you had no interest in becoming His disciple. And you're dismissing Him now."

John, how am I doing that? I love Jesus. He's forgiven my sins. I am His disciple! How am I dismissing Him now?

"Don't you see? You've been summoned by God to become who you are, by God's grace a bearer of His image called to adore Jesus by revealing His grace-filled heart to others. That is true greatness. And it brings with it the happiness of Jesus, the joy of the Trinity. But you are displaying the relational nature of Satan through your attitude toward your friend.

"Yes, you could tell your friend that you would appreciate his exploring you. But know there is a deeper, a greater desire within you. You belong to Jesus. He sees you. He hears you. You want to reveal Him to others, even to those who hurt you badly.

"My soon-to-be-mature friend—God *will* complete the work He has begun—what are you doing? You don't need a friend to show loving interest in you before you're able to offer love. Jesus loves you; He loved you long before you gave Him a kind thought. Go and do likewise. Love your friend with the better love of Jesus. Know who you are: a lover of God and a lover of people because you are loved by God."

Let's back up a bit. Who are we? That's the question, the third question of spiritual theology. Everyone asks it, in one way or another. As a kid, many times I would look into a mirror and ask out loud, "Who is that person?" At the time, I wasn't sure whom I was addressing. I suspect now it might have been God. To my ten-year-old ears, He was silent. The best answer I could come up with was, "That's me."

But that answer brought no settled clarity. The dialogue between me and my image in the mirror would continue. "No, that's not me. I'm not in the mirror. I'm here. I'm me. So who is that?" I'd then go on for five minutes or more, eventually giving up on finding an answer, muttering, "I have no idea what I'm talking about," then running off to play outside.

Small wonder, I suppose, that years later I chose to study psychology. I was an introspective kid. Sunday school and youth group provided no answers to my question. Perhaps psychology would.

Two years into my graduate studies in clinical psychology, I was disillusioned. Neither Freud, Rogers, Skinner, nor more up-to-date theorists of human nature with its problems and available remedies, answered my question. *Who am I? Who are you? Who are we?* I didn't know. But I sensed there was an answer, and I knew it lay in a deeper place than secular wisdom could reach.

Toward the end of my graduate studies, I came across a strong sentence written by Lewis Sperry Chafer, a highly respected theologian. He stated that *no greater revelation about the nature of human beings has ever been given than what the Bible declares, that we bear the image of God.*

A light flickered on in my darkness. Was I hearing God's answer to the question? Since I was a child, I had heard that humans were created in God's image, but it never occurred to me that the idea was important—until now! Was God telling me who I was? Was He telling everyone who would listen, who had ears to hear, the answer to the big question that, for me, had so long remained unanswered? What did it mean, that together we bear the image of God?

Two ideas have taken shape in my understanding since those early days. One, that each of us is a *gendered* image-bearer, a man or woman created by God to uniquely reflect something literally glorious about the way God relates. And two, that the God whose image we bear is a *relational* God, a Trinity of three divine Persons, each one relating with a better kind of love that is worlds different from the way we all naturally relate.

As those two truths developed in my mind, I heard what I now believe is God's answer to question 3. In its short form, the answer is: *We are relational persons with a potential waiting to be realized.* A little longer version would be:

> We are relational persons, created to know joy in knowing God, male and female bearers of God's relational image, with the potential to put Jesus on display as masculine men and feminine women, a potential always waiting to be further realized in this life.

Exactly what does it mean to say that we bear God's image, that the person you see in the mirror, the spouse and children you live with, the friends you know, the grocery store clerk you smile at as you pay your bill, and everyone else is "created for greatness and summoned to it"? The potential for *relational* greatness can be realized because we bear God's image. As image-bearers of the three-Person God who by definition is relational, we have been created with four capacities that when properly exercised make it possible to realize our potential to resemble God by how we love. (These four capacities suggest, I should point out, what it means to bear God's image.

What it means to be a *gendered* image-bearer, a vitally important matter, is unpacked in my earlier book *Fully Alive: A Biblical Vision of Gender That Frees Men and Women to Live beyond Stereotypes*, published by Baker Books. I refer you to that book for an extensive discussion of what it means to be God-revealing masculine men and feminine women.)

As bearers of God's image:

- We are capable of *knowing* God well enough to enjoy Him, all three Persons, more than we enjoy anyone or anything else, and therefore to want nothing greater than to put Jesus on display by how we relate, even in the middle of disappointment, heartache, failure, disease, injustice, or loneliness. Who are we? *We are lovers because we're loved.*

- We are capable of *believing* God so that when prayers go unanswered, when dreams shatter, when all felt sense of His presence, even His existence, vanishes, we remain convinced that He is and that He is good. That is the truth. Who are we? *We are truth-tellers who believe that what Jesus came to tell us is true.*

- We are capable of *choosing* to obey the Father by displaying to others the relational nature of His Son, even when disobedience would make our lives easier or more immediately satisfying. The power to make that choice arises from a previous faith-based choice to discover happiness in delighting God. Who are we? *We are volitional beings who find the joy we were created to know by freely following the way of Jesus.*

- We are capable of *experiencing* God's presence, of knowing with strongly felt certainty that He is with us, whether in bright mornings or during dark nights. We live with the confidence that we experience God most richly to the degree we express Him most fully. Who are we? *We are glad followers of Jesus on the narrow road to joy.*

A spouse hurts you. A child breaks your heart. A friend betrays you. A critic slams you. If you saw yourself as a well-loved lover, a teller of the truth about God, an uncoerced Christian freely choosing to obey God as a disciple on the narrow road to joy, how would you respond? The question cannot always be answered with a to-do list, with specific instructions to follow. Persons who identify themselves as developing "little Christs" would be eager to obey practical moral principles, but even more so they would search for their passionate yearning to reveal the better love of Christ to the other, a yearning that lies in the center of every Christian's heart. God's Spirit would honor that search and nudge the seeker in directions that might be costly but would be obviously right.

Satan, however, will not keep quiet. He seizes the opportunity of my being failed by others to nudge me in a very different direction. And to up the odds that I will be drawn to his evil, he provides his deceptively appealing answer to question 3. If who I am is not a *relational* person with potential waiting to be realized but rather a *needy* person who justly lives to have my needs met, then the devil's counsel will seem right and good.

Michael Card put it well. "Part of keeping on the narrow road means keeping an eye out for false prophets. They have the appearance of true sheep outwardly but inwardly they are as ferocious as wolves."[2]

Speaking for the devil but presenting themselves as representing God, false prophets might respond to question 3 with something like this: "Yes, you do bear God's image. You are special to Him. Because you are in relationship with Jesus, as everyone is whether they realize it yet or not, you can expect your heavenly Father will take good care of you. Depend on God to do what He promised to do. Paul told you that 'this same God who takes care of me will supply all your needs from his glorious riches.' And Jesus Himself said that 'live righteously, and he [your heavenly Father] will give you everything you need'" (Phil. 4:19; Matt. 6:33).

Remember how the devil tempted Jesus in the wilderness, appealing to several verses from the Old Testament. If Satan stooped so low as to twist Scripture in an effort to get Jesus offtrack, it's clear he will do the same with us, with more hope of success. Of course God will supply everything we need, *but everything we need to advance His kingdom, not to enjoy a pleasant life.*

The short form of Satan's answer to question 3 might be expressed as follows: "We are needy persons whose needs must be met for us to feel happy." A longer version adds detail:

> We are individual persons, loved by God as men and women who bear His image, with personal needs that must be met by others in a way that lets us feel good about ourselves and our lives. Only then will we find joy in following Jesus as we live our lives.

Personal needs? I need a loving spouse, well-behaved children, a supportive family, a good job that pays decently, good health, successful ministry, relaxing vacations—let's see. I'm sure I have more needs. God wants me happy. So of course He'll meet every one, or at least enough for me to feel good about myself and my life.

Through his willingly deceived minions (I'm referring to false prophets), Satan goes on. Who are we? As image-bearers:

- We are capable of *knowing* God well enough to trust that His love will provide for every need we want satisfied. *We are loved individuals who can count on God to make our lives comfortable.*
- We are capable of *believing* God, persuaded that the truth of His goodness guarantees that the blessings we ask for will be given. *We are truth-tellers, claiming the truth that every difficulty opens the door to greater blessings that make us happy.*
- We are capable of *choosing* to live in a way that results in divine favor, in God transforming our lives into a happy experience.

We are volitional persons, free to make choices that lead to consistently answered prayer.

- We are capable of *experiencing* God, of feeling His comforting presence so that we never sink into dark nights of loneliness, doubt, or confusion. *We are happy followers of Jesus on a road that always leads us into pleasant circumstances.*

Satan's twisted theology feeds the self-centeredness that "causes quarrels . . . and fights" in our relationships (James 4:1 ESV). I require that others treat me well. The result? I "covet and cannot obtain" (v. 2 ESV). His input leads me to define who I am as a needy individual entitled to getting what I need, from others and from life, to provide me with second thing happiness. Satan never aims higher.

But when I hear God's answer to question 3, when I embrace the truth that

- I am a bearer of God's relationally loving image;
- everything I need to realize my destiny to love like Jesus has been met in Jesus;
- because there is no greater way to live, I want nothing more than to love with the better love of Jesus, to become a "little Christ"; and
- a civil war rages in my soul, between the story God is telling and the story Satan is telling;

then I will know what Thomas Chalmers spoke of as "the expulsive power of a new affection."[3] I will *want* to enter the battle for a better love. I will *want* to live congruently with the divine nature of outwardness that now resides in the depths of who I truly am. I will *want* to walk the narrow road that leads me to relational life.

Despise me. Criticize me. Misunderstand me. Ignore me. Reject me. Judge me. Do your worst to me, *and if I know who I am*, I will be aware that a potential to love like Jesus is alive in my soul, waiting to be fully realized. I will enter the battle for a better love, recognizing God's voice and following Him, and recognizing Satan's voice and resisting everything he says.

But it's clear I have a long way to go. I often don't love well. What's gone wrong?

16

Question 4
What's Gone Wrong?

A recovery of the old sense of sin is essential to Christianity. Christ takes it for granted that men are bad. Until we really feel this assumption of His to be true, though we are part of the world He came to save, we are not part of the audience to which His words are addressed.

C. S. Lewis[1]

Lewis speaks of the old sense of sin. Is there a new sense, a new way to understand what's gone wrong with us that's more in fashion today? I think there is. Satan is at it again.

The enemy of everything good comes up with a bad answer to all the good questions we need to ask. If believed, his appealing but poison-laced answers nudge us off the narrow road to abundant life and get us happily walking the broad road to a wasted life.

Notice a crucial point implied by Lewis: if we're to hear Christ's answers to the questions that matter most, we must not only *agree* with Him that we're bad but also *feel* that we're bad. It's easier to feel that we're misunderstood, or unappreciated for all the good we do, or sympathized with too little for all the wounds we've suffered and the mistreatment we've endured. Of course we sometimes do bad things. But don't blame us. Can't anyone see we're hurting?

In our therapeutic culture, we've come to believe we're more insecure than wicked. Feelings of rejection and inadequacy define us, not evil. That's a lie, but Satan has the advantage. *Lies are more easily believed than truth.*

When we buy into the notion that what's most wrong with us is the damage we've suffered from life, our spirit of entitlement blooms quickly like a flowering weed that's bound to wither but only after a long, robust life. We believe we're owed whatever we need to repair the damage. It might be an exciting experience of God's presence, or maybe a better job or a better spouse.

Jesus thinks differently. He tells us we're bad, self-centered to the core, in dire need of forgiveness and formation. Tolerance, understanding, and repair will not do what's needed for us to really live. But lies are more easily believed than truth. We prefer hell's foolishness to heaven's wisdom.

Agreeing with the Bible's answer to question 4 is one thing. Feeling the truth of its answer is another. The unholy trinity—the world, the flesh, and the devil—has gotten us so preoccupied with what's wrong in the world and in other people that we pay little attention to what may be wrong in us. The *pain* we feel in our hearts brought on by the world we live in feels so much deeper than any *evil* that might exist in our souls. It is only right, even moral, to relieve our pain rather than face our sin. Or so we think.

A new sense of sin justifies the effort to do whatever is needed to feel better. That new sense defines our worst problem as weakened self-love, the result of others not loving us well. As fallen people, we believe that our worst failure is to count ourselves unworthy of the love we need. We therefore sin against ourselves by not being committed to our own self-interest. It is now moral to live "authentically," authentic to whomever we feel ourselves to be. This new sense of sin closes our ears to hearing the old story of Jesus, the story of sinners saved by grace, the good and true story of God.

I sometimes wonder if Satan cherishes no greater ambition than to sell us on an answer to question 4 that does away with the need for repentance. I imagine he takes evil pleasure when we think we're repenting of sin but are really justifying our failure. "I admit I was wrong. I ask your forgiveness," we say. But to ourselves, we add, *But I've been wronged by others more severely than I've wronged anyone. It's the others who have more reason than I to repent.*

Satan is artfully tricky. I've heard him whisper to me, "Your sin against another has brought you trouble. Repent in order to enjoy a less troubled life." If I listen to him, my repentance then becomes manipulatively self-serving, with no sorrowful awareness of having committed a capital offense against God. Restored intimacy with Jesus that frees me to display His forgiving love to others is not the point of false repentance. False repentance is designed to restore a better life for *me*.

Satan finds as much delight in false repentance as in no repentance. You're familiar with false repentance. So am I. Our choices have made us miserable. We think our choices were sinful *because* they made us miserable. So we repent, with no higher goal than to experience relief from trouble. Thomas Watson, a Puritan writer in the 1600s, exposes the falseness of false repentance in a striking thought: "If pain and trouble were sufficient to repentance, then the damned in hell should be most penitent, for they are most in anguish."[2]

Let me here insert a parenthetical thought. Watson's book *The Doctrine of Repentance* is a searing exposure of sin that false repentance fails to take into account. To modern ears, the book can be discouraging, even oppressive in its understanding of sin. And yet he ends his introduction by signing himself as "The well-wisher of your happiness."[3] He seems to think that a deep sense of one's own sinfulness doesn't eliminate joy but rather releases it.

Puritans are unfairly caricatured as enemies of happiness. One critic who believed Puritans were killjoys remarked, "The Puritans hated bear-hunting, not because it gave pain to the bear, but because it gave pleasure to the spectators."[4] But Richard Sibbes, a noted Puritan, wrote, "The end (goal) of the ministry is not to tyrannize over people's souls, to sting and vex them, but . . . *to be helpers of their joy; that is to help their . . . happiness, which is here termed joy.*"[5]

As a hopefully modern Puritan, I believe that a sorrowfully felt awareness of sin as being a wicked affront to God leads to true repentance, which is the only pathway to enjoying the happiness of Jesus. A condemning answer to question 4 opens the door to a liberating realization of joy. We can then live authentically as who we really are: forgiven sinners on our way to becoming Spirit-formed lovers. A fuller answer to how feeling our badness leads to the experience of joy awaits in the next several chapters. It's there the good news is seen to be really good.

David committed adultery. He sinned against Bathsheba by using her for his own pleasure. He sinned against her husband by murdering him. He arranged for Uriah to be killed to protect himself from shame. But when David came to his senses and confessed his sin, he acknowledged to God that "Against you, you only, have I sinned and done what is evil in your sight" (Ps. 51:4 ESV). I wonder if Bathsheba's father or Uriah's brother would have agreed with David.

The enormity of David's sin against God did not minimize the evil of his sin against the woman he violated or the man he murdered. It rather revealed that beneath the wickedness of adultery and murder lay a more loathsome evil, a proud inclination to serve one's own interests above all others, including God's, and to listen to Satan's treacherous foolishness instead of God's loving wisdom.

Within the last two weeks, with new eyes I have seen a commitment to my felt well-being that has survived countless efforts at repentance. I realize now that what I too often thought was true repentance only ignited a determined resolve to never again indulge a favorite sin. It didn't work. Why? Have I been depending on personal effort rather than spiritual power? Is the Spirit's power released only through true repentance, which is brokenness over sin against God rather than anguish over pain in myself? Will I be able to consistently resist temptation only when I enter the battle against sin in order to love well?

Recovering the old sense of sin enables true repentance. The effect of true repentance is not stronger determination to never sin but rather to eagerly anticipate more joy in resisting temptation. Living life on the narrow road is becoming more appealing; I find myself gratefully receiving as a gift the opportunity to love well and resist sin.

Repentance that releases joy and provides freedom requires that we understand the sin that demands repentance. We need to hear God's answer to question 4: *What's gone wrong?* But we will not hear His answer until we clearly see that His answers to the first three questions compel us to ask the fourth with the utmost seriousness. A brief review:

Question 1: *Who is God?* Answer: a party happening! He is a relational God who thoroughly enjoys His three-Person community because He relates with love.

Question 2: *What is God up to?* Answer: He is displaying His suffering, sacrificial love by inviting us to the party! He is leading us to dance in rhythm with His divine relational nature, forming us through seasons of blessing and suffering to love like Jesus.

Question 3: *Who are we?* Answer: men and women who bear God's relational image and are therefore equipped with the capacity to enjoy God and love like Jesus.

So, we then assume, all is good. God is good. His plan is good. And we have the capacity to be good. *But we're not good.* Something has gone wrong. What is it?

Why does sin so often seem attractive, somehow necessary to my felt well-being, to the satisfaction of what I believe I most want and need? Sexual addiction, compulsive under- and overeating, self-protection against further rejection, grudge-holding that seems justified: Why can what I know to be wrong feel so right? The answer? *I long to feel what I was created to feel more than I want to be who I was created to be.* Feelings then trump truth as the motivation for the choices I make.

I feel incomplete. I *am* complete in Christ, but I don't experience myself as complete. Like Paul, I groan. I long for a fully satisfying experience that is not yet available. Sometimes I hurt. I worry. I feel afraid. Anger, even bitterness, seethes within me. I often feel inadequate. And I know it's more than a feeling. I *am* inadequate. I'm dependent on strength I don't have, on resources not within me.

So I set about to come at this sad state of affairs with God's help if He provides it—and without His help if He doesn't. I raise my fist in God's face. I cannot bear my sadness. *God, can't You see that? Don't You care? I cannot endure my loneliness. You must come through for me.* My desperation becomes a demand. My worst problem is pain. God should do something about it.

Requiring God to relieve my pain seems so reasonable. When I was writhing in agony over a kidney stone, a doctor kindly assured me, "We have more medicine than you have pain." But when I come to God more aware of soul pain than of anything else, He says, "Repent!" Of what?

Christ's first recorded words as an adult were, "Repent of your sins and turn to God" (Matt. 3:2). Turn to God for what? I want relief. He offers forgiveness. His final instruction to the disciples was to tell everyone, "There is forgiveness of sins for all who repent" (Luke 24:47). Is that what I most want? Do I realize forgiveness is what I most need?

I will not welcome Christ's promise of forgiveness until I feel more sorrow over my sin than anguish over my pain. Listen to Paul begin to unpack the good news of Jesus in Romans. "For the wrath of God is revealed from heaven against . . ." (Rom. 1:18 ESV).

Against what? The cancer that my most recent blood test indicates might still be in my body? The distress you feel in your marriage? Your heartbreak over a son or daughter? An ongoing struggle with depression? A failed ministry?

God weeps when we weep. He can be touched with our feelings of weakness and sorrow. He is not out of touch with our painful reality. (See Heb. 4:15 in the KJV, NIV, ESV, and MSG. Each version says it differently. Together they make it clear that God hurts with us.) But God *relates* to our pain even as He is *angry* at our sin. He won't condemn us. Jesus was condemned in our place. But He is still angry over our sin. He hates sin because it blocks the joy He went to great lengths to make available to us.

We must be clear on this. The end of pain is promised—*later*. Repentance of sin is required *now*. Why? Because "the wrath of God is revealed from heaven *against all ungodliness and unrighteousness*" (Rom. 1:18 ESV). Our woundedness draws out His compassion. Our waywardness offends His holiness.

Through Paul, I hear God providing a clear summary of what's wrong in us.

- *Ungodliness*: a denial of who God is, the source of all that is good, the supply of everything our hearts desire; this denial leads us to look for happiness in whatever feels immediately good.
- *Unrighteousness*: a refusal to both supremely value and deeply trust the good God is up to, forming us to relate like Jesus as we walk the narrow road through life to *life*.

Our continuing ungodliness and unrighteousness lead us onto the broad road where we fail to realize our potential as bearers of God's image, people who were created to enjoy God by relating to Him and others in rhythm with His divine nature. True answers to the first three questions—Who is God? What is He up to? Who are we?—will not lead us to share in the happiness of Jesus if we believe Satan's false answer to question 4. Let me illustrate.

Lauren (not her real name) was sexually abused as a child. As an adult, she now wears a protective crust around her wounded heart. A Christian woman, she wants to love like Jesus but she is afraid of more pain. Her fear has hardened into a demand: *I will not be so badly hurt again.* That demand, though unobserved by her, has numbed her tender heart. *I can't love. It's not in me. I won't risk the hurt I fear.*

Yet the divine nature is lodged in her soul. She may be incapable of relating to another with the confidence that she will not be hurt. But, like Jesus, she is capable of relating to another with a vision of who that other could become, and with the confidence that she can encourage that vision in another by entering the battle for a better love, a love that gives even when it suffers, a love that delights the Father because it reveals the character of His Son.

I am no different than Lauren. For different reasons and in different ways, I grieve and quench God's Spirit. A residual ungodliness and unrighteousness, the sin that the apostle John says is still in me (see 1 John 1:8), at times continues to block the release of the Spirit's power to *trust* God (godliness) and to *obey* God (righteousness)—to realize that there really is no other way to be happy in Jesus.

What's gone wrong? What is the core problem in me that only Jesus can deal with? What is it that when seen and confessed frees me to truly repent?

Satan's answer: *suffering.* "That's your worst problem. Trust God to relieve your pain, to straighten out your difficult circumstances. Repent of your presumed unworthiness to be happy that keeps you from taking care of yourself. Only then will you experience the happiness you deserve to feel. Protect yourself from further pain as best you can. Pursue whatever helps you feel better. Live authentically as a person properly committed to your own felt well-being. It is God's will."

God's answer: *sin*. "That's your worst problem. Trust Me to forgive you. I will. Trust Me to change you. I will. Enter the battle *between* the self-centeredness still in you that I hate because I love you *and* the sacrificial love My Spirit has birthed in your inmost being that I love because it defines who I am. Repent of your sin of self-centeredness, relational sin, the failure to relate like My Son because relief means more to you than holiness. Do not demand relief from your pain. Turn to Me. Learn to love like My Son. You will know His joy. I promise."

God, I hear You. I agree with You. My problem is sin. I can't deal with it on my own. I'm not even sure that I feel my sin to be as bad as You say it is. Please, tell me clearly. Lay it out for me. What is the solution?

That's question 5, and Satan has another bad answer for it. We need to hear God's answer. But before moving on to question 5, I want to again highlight the sin we most often fail to recognize in ourselves, the sin we commit every day: *relational sin*.

Phil's wife doesn't express much interest when he shares his excitement about a rich insight the Lord gave him from a difficult text. He feels disappointed in her, and personally undervalued when she responds with a polite smile and merely says, "I'm glad you enjoy your time in the Bible."

It doesn't occur to him that her bland response might reveal that she feels required by Phil to prop up his ego. Or perhaps she would love to feel his passion directed toward her. It could be she feels so intimidated by his grasp of Scripture that she wonders if he sees her as shallow.

Phil could ask, "Honey, I'd love to know what happens in you when I tell you about something I saw in Scripture that excites me."

Instead he backs away from her with poorly concealed disgust. *That is relational sin.*

As a little girl, Haley was abandoned by her father and tolerated by her mother. She accepted Jesus as her Savior during her college years. At age thirty-two, her dream came true: a good Christian man proposed to her. Two weeks before the wedding he died in a car accident. Her loneliness was unbearable. She felt defined by the ache in her heart. When friends moved toward her with compassion she could talk only of her sorrow. Her friends soon tired of the "pull" they felt from her to admire her noble perseverance through a kind of loneliness that few ever felt. *Her "pull" was relational sin.*

In the thirty-three years of His life in this world Jesus never failed to display the glory of holy love by the way He related, no matter what He endured or how He felt. No day passes without you and me falling short of the relational glory of God. Jesus had no cause to repent. We do, every day.

17

Question 5

What Has God Done about Our Problem?

> Awakening from this dream, he was overwhelmed by a feeling of
> great sadness. It seemed that he had spent his life in a worthless
> and senseless manner; he retained nothing vital, nothing in any
> way precious or worthwhile. He stood alone, like a shipwrecked
> man on the shore.
>
> Herman Hesse[1]

Siddhartha, the main character in Hesse's novel referred to above, faces a dreadful reality. In his dream, the songbird that sings to him every morning sings no more. The songbird has become mute. There is no music to hear.

Siddhartha awakens to the realization that everything he knew to be good and meaningful has died. There was no song to sing. Happiness has vanished. Hesse tells us that the man is disconsolate, without hope, and with slumping shoulders he walks away from the garden where he once felt pleasure, knowing he would never return. The bird in the garden would never sing again. "He was finished with that. That also died in him. That same night Siddhartha left his garden and the town and never returned."[2]

If we're fortunate, if God deals with us in severe mercy, we reach a point in our lives where we can no longer find the happiness we want in the familiar, in all the good things that life provides. We realize we're at a crossroads. Either we will spend our remaining days in misery or we will come to know the happiness of Jesus, a happiness different from the kind we normally seek. God speaks of leading His people into a valley of trouble and then opening their eyes to see that it is a gateway to hope (see Hos. 2:15). When the songbird we know can no longer sing, our only hope is to hear a new song by a new songbird. The inconsolable longing buried deep in our souls beneath the happiness we once found in satisfying lesser desires is being exposed, the longing into which only Jesus can speak.

Indulge a moment of fancy. Suppose Blaise Pascal, the French philosopher, happened to be walking with Siddhartha as he leaves his garden. Pascal has explored the human condition as few others have. He once wrote, "to realize our misery and know nothing of God is mere despair."[3] In Jesus Christ, he added, "we find both human misery and God."[4] I imagine he might say to Siddhartha what he wrote to all of us:

> It is quite certain that there is no good without the knowledge of God; that the closer one comes, the happier one is and the further away one goes, the more unhappy one is.[5]

Envision a second great thinker joining the conversation, Jacques Ellul. His words to Siddhartha might well be these:

> The hope of Jesus Christ is never a dash of pepper or a spoonful of mustard. It is bread and wine, the essential and basic food itself,

without which there is only the delirium of knowledge and an illusion of action.[6]

Bread and wine. Why would Ellul not symbolize the hope of Jesus Christ by offering steak and potatoes to a desperately hungry man? Perhaps a slice of apple pie to add pleasure to nutrition? No, and here's why. Offering bread and wine would be seizing a unique opportunity. *When every source of happiness other than God Himself fails to deliver, when the songbird we've counted on for music can no longer sing, it is then we are best positioned to enjoy bread and wine as a nourishing meal.*

Bread: the symbol of the body of Jesus once broken so brutally that all the nerve endings designed to receive pleasure delivered only pain. Wine: the symbol of the blood of Jesus once poured out, leaving Him emptied of every good thing in life except love. Jesus was punished for our wickedness and killed by His own arrangement so that you and I could be welcomed into the divine community, made alive with divine love that we can now display to others. And now, the happiness that never fails when all other happiness is taken away, the happiness of knowing God personally, emerges in our souls when we reveal God relationally. *The answer to Siddhartha's problem is bread and wine.*

God's answer to our problem is the death of Jesus. What has He done about our problem? *He killed His Son.* But the death of Jesus is experienced as powerless, irrelevant, and of no practical use to us if we're searching for happiness in fulfilling relationships or a generous income or excellent health or successful ministry—all second things that produce second thing happiness. We want the familiar songbird of blessings to keep singing.

God finds our desires too weak. We find God uncooperative. We pray for a better job, better health, a better marriage, better friends—all good prayers, but not when there are none that aim higher. In this life, Jesus promises none of the second things we pray for, though He often provides many. He offers what He thinks is better: the guaranteed opportunity to know joy in our thirsty souls by knowing God intimately, by joining the dance of the Trinity as we reveal to others the plot of the story God is telling. And yet I struggle to believe that Jesus is offering something better. Why? Why do I want a better job and better health and better family life and better community with friends more than I want to love others with a better love?

Am I hearing Satan sounding like a songbird? Have I been lulled into enjoying the happiness available when my life goes well to such a degree that I have little interest in discovering the happiness that comes from loving well? If so, God's good news wrapped up in the death of Jesus will not speak into my felt reality. When my songbird is singing the tune of continued blessings, I'm in danger of listening to no other music. And when that songbird goes mute and I want nothing more than to hear the tune of better times again, the gospel of Jesus will either mean nothing to me or I will pervert it and live in false hope that Jesus will reliably satisfy my weak desires.

It would be wise to ask yourself what songbird has gone mute in your life. What good thing in your life that you looked to for happiness, perhaps a spouse, child, or friend, now brings only pain? Like countless others, perhaps you feel like Siddhartha, shipwrecked and standing alone. If so, don't retreat into self-protective numbness. Feeling your pain opens the door to either despair or hope. And then to find hope you must eat the bread and drink the wine.

In my seventy-plus years, many times I've felt myself drowning in deep waters of heartbreak and failure and walking through fire that threatened to weaken, even destroy, my faith. A thousand times I've asked, is God *really* good? I feel so unheard, unhelped. *Does He care that I'm hurting so badly, struggling so greatly? Does He even notice?*

In moments of intentionally opening myself to feel my trouble, not numbing it, I hear Him say, *Fear not, for I have redeemed you.* I know His words are supposed to make me feel better, to help me rest in the middle of my difficulties. But I want the familiar songbird to sing again, to lift my heart with restored blessings. And yet my prayers go unanswered. Bad times stay bad. In church I sing, "O the cross, the wonderful cross," and I sense a faint stirring of hope that dies when the song ends.

God continues to speak. *I have called you by name. You are Mine.* Then why doesn't He treat me better? Why won't He answer my prayers for good things to happen that would make me happy? God's words can sound more religious than real, sweet but not substantial. I need a really good meal. He offers bread and wine.

But then I remember God's answer to question 4. He thinks my worst problem, a problem that destroys all hope of true joy, is *not* the absence of good things coming toward me but something bad within me—not heartbreak but stubbornness, a false understanding of what brings joy that justifies my self-centered demand that life go well for me and that I be treated well by others. As I reflect on God's answer to question 4, I wonder what *might* happen if I repented—truly repented—of my demand that the songbird sing again, that I find happiness in a source other than the death of Jesus?

What *could* happen if I risked believing that the happiness I most long for is really available in Jesus, not in earthbound blessings that come my way but in the heaven-sent life He gives? What *would* happen if I staked my entire hope of happiness on God's love and on the opportunity to love like Jesus? Have I been building the house of my life on sand when Jesus has supplied a rock, a solid foundation that will keep my life from collapsing?

I begin to hear God singing, "When you pass through the waters, I will be with you; and through the rivers, they shall not overwhelm you; when you walk through fire you shall not be burned, and the flame shall not consume you" (Isa. 43:2 ESV).

But still I resist. Floodwaters have reached my neck. Fire is burning my house. I'm scared. I'm mad. I'm hurt. I'm not yet ready to join heaven's choir in singing with joy about the Lamb who was slain. God promises to be with me when I pass through deep waters. Couldn't He lead me on dry ground to a pleasant meadow? He tells me the fire will not burn me. But I'm already burning. Why won't He just put out the fire? *No, God, You're not getting through to me. I'm not yet delighting in Your answer to question 5.* I feel shipwrecked. I am Siddhartha. God sent Pascal and Ellul to speak to me, but their words have yet to fill me with joy.

At this point, it might be good to remind you of something I said earlier. This book is a story unfolding. I did not begin writing with a well-developed message that I was confident I could articulate. I expect to complete the last chapter with more loose ends hanging in my mind than in yours. Coming up with each sentence feels more like an adventure on an important journey than a carefully organized lecture.

Even now, as I'm writing this chapter, a verse just came to mind that I had no previous thought to mention. It's near the beginning of Paul's most complete teaching about what happened when Jesus died. I've *read* it a thousand times. I'm *hearing* it now.

> For I am not ashamed of the gospel, for it is the power of God for salvation to everyone who believes. (Rom. 1:16 ESV)

Another translation says it this way:

> For I am not ashamed of this Good News about Christ. It is the power of God at work, saving everyone who believes.

Two questions immediately come to mind. Saving everyone from what? Certainly not from deep waters and scorching flames, perhaps

185

through them but not *from* them. Then from what? As preachers from an earlier generation used to say, we've been saved from the penalty of sin, we're being saved from the power of sin, and we will be saved from the presence of sin. Add those three thoughts together and you come up with this: *the power of God is at work, saving everyone who believes in Christ from the eternal penalty of self-centeredness and releasing them into radical other-centeredness, loving like Jesus.* The death of Jesus saves us from slavery to selfishness so that we can now enter the battle for a better love until the day the battle is forever and completely won.

A second question: Is Paul concerned that some Christians might actually be ashamed of the gospel? I think so. But why would that be? Is it possible that *I've* been ashamed of the gospel, perhaps without knowing it? Am I still? Of course I value the death of Jesus as my already-paid ticket to heaven. And I should. I'm grateful. But now, in this life with all its disappointments and heartaches, has His crucifixion become irrelevant? If so, is it because His death guarantees only that my soul will get better when what I want more is that my life get better?

The gospel of Jesus that centers on the death of Jesus meant everything to Paul, from the time of his conversion on the Damascus road to his final days in a Roman dungeon. And yet for those thirty-plus years in between, his life was one long shipwreck. His life did not get better. Things got worse. "Pressed on every side," Paul was literally shipwrecked, stoned, hated, scorned, and devastated by some Christians who put their trust in a more user-friendly gospel (see 2 Cor. 4:8–9; Gal. 1).

And yet he was *not* crushed, *not* driven to despair, *never* abandoned by God, and *not* destroyed. But why? "Through suffering . . . the life of Jesus" became always more visible in his life to all who had eyes to see (2 Cor. 4:10). Paul was overwhelmed, not by the deep waters he traveled through but by the privilege of displaying Jesus to others, a privilege made possible through the death of Jesus. He was consumed, not by the fire of troubles but by the fire of God's Spirit calling him to the faith and providing the power required to battle for a better love (see 1 Pet. 1:6–7).

I want to live a cross-shaped life, a life that frees me from working to bolster my self-esteem through other people's approval. I no longer want to feel that my life is too hard to live. I don't want to live discouraged and bitter as a shipwrecked man alone on a deserted island with no hope of rescue. I want to welcome whatever comes my way, whether wonderful blessings or heartbreaking trials, as "an opportunity for great joy," the opportunity to display the love of Jesus that advances others' well-being at any cost to my own (see James 1:2). *I want to live the abundant life of loving like Jesus, the truly good life, available to me and to you through the death of Jesus.*

But isn't that life made possible *through the resurrection* of Jesus, not His crucifixion? It's true, of course, and profoundly true, that if Jesus were not resurrected His death would be a tragedy without meaning. But notice this: Jesus announced *it is finished* not after His resurrection but while He was still hanging on the cross, moments before His physical death when He released His spirit, and moments after the three hours of darkness when He experienced soul death, abandoned by God.

At exactly that time, something was finished. What was it? By living in this world for thirty-three years, He revealed how bearers of God's image were designed to relate. By dying, He accomplished so much more:

- Sin's penalty was paid.
- The devil was defeated.
- Suffering love was fully revealed.

The Lion will one day roar and declare, "Look, I am making everything new!" (Rev. 21:5), but only because the Lamb was slaughtered. In John's vision, heaven's choir, after the resurrection, sang "Worthy is the Lamb who was slain" (5:12 ESV). Why not sing "Worthy is the Lion who was resurrected"? The choir is celebrating that sin's penalty is paid, Satan's power is undone, and divine love, suffering love, is revealed, *all in the death of Jesus.*

Do I celebrate God's forgiving, powerful, suffering love more than the second thing blessings He provides? Do I celebrate the devil's defeat by trusting that he no longer has controlling power in my life? Do I celebrate suffering as a glad opportunity to put Jesus on display without demanding relief? And do I celebrate the power of Christ's resurrection to battle for a better love, a power released in me only when I eat the bread and drink the wine?

Can you hear it? The divine songbird is singing. *He is not mute and never will be.* The Spirit's sweet song reveals the answer to question 5: What has God done about the one problem we have that ruins our joy? Answer? *It is finished!*

We are, in this moment and in every moment, in relationship with God. We are freed from the devil's power that aims to keep us living for self-glorification, for feeling good through any means necessary. And we have been given the chance to live, not the worthless and senseless life of Siddhartha but the eternally meaningful life of telling God's story while we live in this world. Spiritual blessings all, in heavenly places but given to us on earth.

When I stand before the cross and realize what happened because Jesus suffered, if I am not moved to the core of my being it may be because I'm listening to Satan's answer to question 5, an answer that I can tell is off-key but one I still find appealing. His answer is sometimes heard from pulpits:

Yes, celebrate Jesus. Celebrate His example. Do your best to love like Him, and your life will go well. Speak little about sin and self-centeredness. Such talk can be unnecessarily discouraging. Of course you make mistakes. God knows you're not perfect. But speak much of His love. The work of Jesus is nearly finished. By living well and dying well, He began the good work of showing you how to love. Complete the work now by living well and loving well, according to His teaching. Follow the principles He taught. Make social justice, not pie-in-the-sky hope in the middle of ongoing injustice, a priority in your mission. And the abundant life of blessings will be yours to enjoy. Trust Him to give you that life. It is the *Christian* life.

Satan always lies, but he is a clever liar. He seductively deceives us by whispering half-truths. Satan does not want us to see all that really happened on Calvary. Did Jesus provide the perfect example of suffering love? Of course! But no one until heaven will ever live up to the standard He set. That is why He died. We are forgiven for falling short of the relational glory of God. The work is finished. The power to be relationally formed like Jesus, though never completely till we see Him in glory, is now available. We can now find joy, true joy, by enduring whatever suffering comes our way as we battle for a better love, knowing every failure to love like Jesus is cause to celebrate His death.

Believing these staggering truths, valuing them above all other truth, is necessary. *Living* these truths requires more. When Jesus was resurrected from His grave and had returned to His throne in heaven, He sent His Spirit to enable us to live these truths. But how does He do that? How does God's Spirit release divine power into our lives, the power to love like Jesus? That is question 6.

The devil is defeated. For now that means he has severe laryngitis but can still squeak out a tune that resonates with our remaining energy of self-centeredness. He manages to sound musical as he sings his lies. We need to hear the sweet song of the Spirit answer our next question.

18

Question 6

How Is the Spirit Working to Implement the Divine Solution to Our Human Problem?

God's purpose is to make the soul great. . . . Oh souls created for greatness and summoned to it—*what are you doing?*

John of the Cross[1]

How does the Holy Spirit lead Jesus followers toward soul greatness? What does it mean to be a great soul? Is that what I most want? How can I know when He is leading me toward that end? What does God's Spirit do to form me into a great soul, a little Christ?

These are not easy questions. And they each flow out from question 6. I've been preparing to write this chapter for more than a month. When I completed the previous chapter and began thinking about this one, I realized with some frustration that I could come up with nothing I wanted to say that felt alive. Of course that troubled me. I had no choice but to wonder if I had any experiential awareness that a divine Person was living in me and doing good things for me and through me.

During these past four weeks, I read, and in some cases reread, a half dozen books by respected scholars who presented their carefully studied understanding of who the Holy Spirit is and how He works in the lives of Jesus followers. The reading has been valuable.

I've been made more aware that the Spirit, one of the three relationally holy members of the Trinity, is Himself a real living Person who is available to me as a counselor, comforter, companion, and conduit of the Father's love and the Son's wisdom. I was directed to Scriptures that assured me nothing I might do, no matter how terrible, would drive Him away. And with fresh awareness I understood that He is carrying out in my life the plan that Christ's death set in motion and that He will provide sustaining hope when that plan seems off course.

I was most impacted by thinking about what it could mean to have an actual relationship with the Spirit. He isn't a mere map with a highlighted route to knowing the Father and Son. Neither is He a distant spiritual celebrity who only inspires me to develop my kingdom-building talents, nor is He a professional coach who offers only advice, never Himself. Perhaps with new eyes I am seeing Him as a very real Person with whom I can relate and realizing that the stronger my relationship with the Spirit the more I will enjoy relationship with the Father and Son. To know one member of the Trinity spills over into knowing the other two.

But I've also come to realize more clearly that developing a relationship with the Spirit would require something of me I feel strangely reluctant to give. *I would need to follow His lead to face both the self-centeredness that corrupts my efforts to love and the intolerable ache in my soul that I prefer to hide beneath a busy life.* So much is wrong in this world and in the church and in me. I want things to be better.

191

Although I teach against it, I would prefer to envision the Christian life as pleasantly fulfilling and meaningfully active in doing good things with little need to examine the *quality* of my love for God or others.

As those thoughts surfaced in my awareness, I felt more than challenged. I was frightened and a bit unnerved. I think that's why, when I sat at my desk and wrote "chapter 18" on the top left corner of my otherwise blank legal pad, nothing more came. The page remained empty. I wanted to go watch television.

Had I grieved the Spirit, perhaps quenched Him? I didn't know. I invited Him, Psalm 139–style, to search my heart, to reveal how I might have offended Him. It was then I felt quietly compelled to pick up a book from my shelves that I had read years ago and remembered as dull. It was written by Thomas Watson, a seventeenth-century Puritan pastor. His book is simply titled *The Doctrine of Repentance*. I mentioned this book before, in chapter 16. I want to briefly refer to it again.

Among his many other insights that gripped me, Watson's understanding of false repentance stood out. Our repentance is false, he suggested, when our desire to get rid of a particular sin is most prompted by the hope of a less difficult life. True repentance grows out of a passionate longing to draw near to God, to see in Him what we want to show others. That distinction between false and true repentance hit home. The book no longer seemed dull.

A few days later I again felt drawn to another book, one I had read several times with appreciation. I grabbed *The Impact of God*, Iain Matthew's short, dense book on the life and thinking of John of the Cross, and eagerly flipped pages to find two quotes that were alive in my mind. One was his strong statement that "God's purpose is to make the soul great." The other was his searching question that I sensed the Spirit was now asking me, "Oh [soul], created for greatness and summoned to it—*what are you doing?*" (Yes, chapter 15 also begins with this same quote. It deserves a second highlight.)

Was the Spirit speaking to me, calling me to look more deeply into what was going on in my soul? My prayer for the Spirit to search my heart, Watson's thoughts on false repentance, and John's worry that souls created for greatness were settling for less—they all came together into a disturbing awareness.

I saw myself as working hard, and I thought nobly, to reduce the mystery of the Spirit (who, like the wind, blows as He wants) into spiritual-sounding steps I could take that would harness His power to cooperate with my agenda. That awareness surprised me. I've long been an anti-step crusader, believing there are no formulas to follow that bring about spiritual maturity. I've strongly spoken against the managed life, the effort to "get it right" so that "life goes well." And now I found myself embracing a well-disguised version of something I've consciously opposed. Let me make clear what I mean.

John of the Cross described his sense of the Spirit's presence as a "'fiesta' in the soul."[2] I had been trying to figure out what I could do to bring that party into my soul. He saw our souls as empty caverns that are deep "because that which can fill them is deep, infinite; and that is God."[3] I recognized my tendency to try to calculate, to know the spiritual disciplines I could follow that would put me in touch with my infinite thirst and persuade the Spirit to fill me. *Relating* with the Spirit was not my interest. *Using* Him was, in order to feel what I longed to feel.

It wasn't happening. If a party was going on in my soul, I couldn't hear the music. I was aware of an ache in my soul, a thirst for water that no one was giving to me. I didn't want to live with an empty soul. I wanted the divine solution to provide an experience that, when I'm thinking clearly, I realize I will never know until heaven.

Am I a spiritual man, a Spirit-filled disciple of Jesus? Ask me that question and most often I will feel immediate discouragement. Why? Could it be that I've been listening to evil lies that I received as spiritual truth? In Western culture—Western *church* culture—Christians have been encouraged to assume that Spirit-filled disciples generally feel pretty good, that the spiritual fruit of love, joy, and peace does away with any ongoing need to struggle against sin and sorrow. Love, we assume, destroys self-centeredness as surely as chemotherapy kills cancer cells. Doesn't it? Joy expels sorrow the way sexual pleasure, at least for a few moments, eliminates relational tension. Or at least it should. And peace leaves no room for worry, much like a financial windfall gets rid of anxiety over bills. Isn't that what it's supposed to do?

But that's broad road thinking. And when self-centeredness is exposed, when relational tensions return, and when anxiety upsets us, Satan seizes his opportunity: "The narrow road is not leading you to life. You want to follow Jesus? You're eager to relate with the Spirit and heed His promptings? How's it working for you?" Our faith wavers and sometimes collapses. Obey God by loving someone who wronged us? Why bother?

To Christians who perhaps unconsciously but intentionally stay so busy that they don't recognize what's going on in their souls, the devil has a different answer to question 6: "You're doing well. You're influencing culture. You're serving the church. You're supporting missions. Don't get muddled with navel-gazing. Keep up the good work. There's no need to worry over your internal world, no need to ask yourself what's happening in your soul or to ask others if they feel loved by you. You are loving well. You're doing fine."

To the most superficial among us, Satan is encouraging. "God wants you to be happy in a life that is going well for you. And when things get hard, think positive thoughts. God will honor your faith by turning things around. You serve a big God. Expect big blessings."

Such a creative and deceptively alluring variety of devilish answers to question 6:

- Try the broad road. The Spirit won't mind. He can do good work there too.
- Live to bring biblical values into your culture. That's what the Spirit is most leading you to do.

- You'll know you're following the Spirit on the narrow road when you're most happy with yourself.

We need to hear God's answer to question 6. It begins with the good news that the third Person of the Trinity supplies both a quietly solid awareness of His *presence* and a freeing realization of His *power* to enable us to fight the battle for a better love.

And it continues with two parts that are made necessary by the problem in our souls: our abiding self-centeredness. God does want His children to be happy, *but with first thing happiness that comes as we are learning to love like Jesus.* And the Spirit is working to implement the divine solution of Christ's death and resurrection in order to slowly, and incompletely till heaven, solve our human problem of self-centeredness that is corrupting our efforts to love. As I now present what I believe to be God's two-part answer to question 6, notice the contrast with each of Satan's lies.

Part 1: The Holy Spirit's presence can be known most richly in our darkness and distress.

Part 2: The Holy Spirit's power can be known most potently in our weakness and failure.

The Holy Spirit's Presence Can Be Known Most Richly in Our Darkness and Distress

Consider Jesus. When did He most need to know the Spirit's presence that assured Him of His Father's love? Remember Gethsemane. In that garden, He keenly felt the darkness of the world's rejection, the darkness of His closest friends' desertion, and the darkness of His mission that meant untold agony.

In that darkness, He addressed God as *Father*, the word that speaks deeply into the reality of relationship. Was Jesus filled with the Spirit even as He experienced the agony of darkness? Could He receive the

195

angel's strengthening because the Spirit was alive in His soul? The morning star of spiritual reality is most visible just before dawn, when the night of spiritual struggle is darkest.

And think of Calvary. Was He living a Spirit-filled life even as He was dying for our sins? He had no awareness of His Father's loving presence during those literally hellish three hours of darkness. Was the Spirit somehow present to Him, focusing His soul on the Father's good purpose? I can't know, but I suspect He was. He was strengthened to endure Gethsemane's agony by an angel. I like to think He was strengthened to endure Calvary's hell by the Spirit. In unmitigated darkness a desperate soul whose heart is right with God can count on the Spirit's endearing and empowering presence, even if unfelt.

Consider Paul. He was pressed on every side, perplexed, hunted down, beaten, shipwrecked—see 2 Corinthians 4:8–9 to read just an incomplete list of all that he suffered. Was Paul walking the narrow road? Was he filled with the Spirit? When he most needed to know the Spirit was alive in his soul, supplying what could sustain him on the narrow road, the Spirit made His presence known to Paul. He knew that his severe hardships and painful emotions provided a dark background on which to display the dazzling light of love: love for God, love for God's message, and love for souls created for greatness and summoned to it (see v. 10).

Talk of the Spirit's life-giving presence is little more than feel-good religious prattle until we embrace life's difficulties and emotional struggles, even hardships severe enough to bring us to the brink of despair, as mysterious opportunities to trust the Spirit within us to accomplish what Christ's crucifixion and resurrection made possible: that we become lovers like Jesus.

Satan is a liar, a damned liar. I use the word with theological accuracy. He wants us to believe a damnable lie, that the Spirit's presence guarantees protection against continuing tough times and painful feelings. God tells us that His Spirit's presence awakens us to an ache in our souls for what is not fully available in this life but also to a hope that survives the hardest of times, the hope of Christ's return tomorrow and the hope that today's battle for a better love is on course. In the middle of life's darkest hours, "overwhelming victory is ours through Christ, who loved us" (Rom. 8:37). The Spirit is present to us and fully alive in us as a Person. Count on it. No, count on Him!

Especially in depths of darkness that requires faith can we develop a solid even if unfelt certainty that God's Spirit is present in us and alive for us, present with divine love and power—a certainty that survives the worst of circumstances and the most severe of disappointments.

The Holy Spirit's Power Can Be Known Most Potently in Our Weakness and Failure

When I feel alive in my blessings, when I'm most aware of my wife's love, when I'm most grateful for restored health, when I'm most excited about my work and ministry, I am most in danger of *not* meaningfully depending on the Spirit's power to love, of assuming that nothing in me needs radical power to radically love.

The Spirit sometimes guides us away from that danger by permitting cherished dreams to shatter. Our souls then ache with an agonizing emptiness that we're helpless to fill. We can numb the feeling of emptiness in any number of ways, some explicitly sinful; but if we choose to embrace its reality, we learn to pray.

Only when desperate thirst cries out from agonizing emptiness, a void we can do nothing to fill, can we pray with single-minded passion, "Holy Spirit, fill me. Fill me with the power to remain on the narrow road. Only then will I be able to fight the battle to love."

It's dependence that makes the difference.

But the Spirit does more. Gently, but not painlessly, He exposes the self-centeredness that soils our best efforts to love. We see the seemingly uncrossable chasm between *relational holiness*, the sacrificing, suffering love of Jesus most fully visible as He hung on the cross, and *relational unholiness*, our way of loving that remains blemished with self-interest. It is then we realize that not only are we helplessly empty but we are also hopelessly broken, unable to love like Jesus without the Spirit's power. Severe words no longer feel too severe. We sing of amazing grace that saved a *wretch* like me. Our therapeutic, politically correct culture thinks it is evil to damage anyone's favorable estimate of themselves. But only in agonizing repentance, true repentance over our failure to love like Jesus, over clearly recognized and sorrowfully confessed relational sin, can we pray with profound dependence, "Holy Spirit, change me. I am forgiven, but I am not yet fully relationally formed like Jesus. May the narrow road squeeze out of me everything that offends You and release the life You've placed in me that delights You."

If we're to hear God's answer to question 6, if we're to know how the Holy Spirit works to make our souls great with relational holiness, we must not look for formulas to follow or manageable steps to take. Instead, we must open ourselves to face reality. *Without the Spirit we will live empty lives; without the Spirit we will have no power to love.* Joy, the happiness of Jesus, will remain out of reach.

Sincere repentance over recognized sinfulness is necessary for salvation, to be forgiven and restored to relationship with God. But walking the narrow road to a life that displays Christ's way of loving to others requires more. Agonizing repentance over blame-worthy relational brokenness *and* painful recognition of despair-worthy relational emptiness *and* immobilizing realization of hope-threatening relational darkness are each, in seasons arranged by God's Spirit, essential for sanctification, for us to be relationally formed with the power to resemble Jesus.

The narrow road is narrow, but it moves us toward the surpassing joy of intimacy with each member of the Trinity.

Together, we can walk that road. Together, we can change. God makes great souls, souls that love greatly, as we live in community with the Trinity and with each other, with fellow travelers on the narrow road. And that brings us to our seventh and final question of spiritual theology: *How can we cooperate, together, with what the Spirit is doing in our lives?*

Once again the devil has an answer that sounds good but never leads us to the kinds of relationships that pour Christ into each other. We'll look for God's answer to question 7 in the next chapter.

19

Question 7

How Can We Cooperate with the Spirit's Work?

I wish we could love as He did—now!

Mother Teresa[1]

Am I a naive ideologue, setting us up for failure by raising the bar too high? No, I don't think so, but the bar is high. God is the one who put it there. And yes, by His standards, in our efforts to love we will fall short every day. The better love I want to battle for is a kind of love that no one but Jesus delivers perfectly. I'm not even certain what a loving response untainted by self-interest would be, especially when a friend irritates me. Thoughts other than loving that friend come easily and quickly to mind.

Am I absurdly unrealistic to think that a woman would experience joyful freedom, along with deep sadness and hurt, if she displayed some approximation of the love of Jesus to a husband who had caused her great heartache? Could a man really enjoy a satisfying but strangely unfamiliar sort of happiness if he moved with genuine (though still imperfect) love toward a cold, unresponsive wife? Would revealing Jesus bring him joy, even if his God-revealing movement toward her never melted the ice covering his wife's heart? To the first question, no. To the second and third, yes.

I want to battle for a better love. I hope you do as well. But the risk is real. "Everyone who wants to live a godly life in Christ Jesus will suffer persecution" (2 Tim. 3:12). Disciples of Jesus will be hurt. The cost is great. *But the gain is greater.* Remember that the cost suffered by Jesus in loving us was great. The gain was infinitely greater. God's love story moved forward, with us now part of the plot.

Your son is sullen and disrespectful. A parent's natural first thought is to decide how best to straighten him out. That's the *first* thing. Is tough love the best strategy? Would counseling work better?

A disciple of Jesus, a true disciple, would think differently. For the parents to cooperate with the Spirit's work *in themselves* would be the first thing. Their son straightening out, though legitimately desired and fervently prayed for, would be a second thing. Engaging the battle to love their son with Jesus-like love, keeping first things first, would provide the most room for the Spirit to answer their second thing prayer, if and when He chose to do so.

But I have to ask again: Is the bar discouragingly high? Is this new way of living a utopian dream that cannot be realized? Spouses hurt each other. Children break the hearts of their parents. Friends get out of sorts with each other. What does it mean—is it even possible—to battle for a better kind of love when relationships are so messy and so often difficult?

It simply cannot be denied: Jesus wants us to give ourselves to others, to risk terrible disappointment and agonizing rejection. We cannot *give* ourselves to others and, at the same time, relate either to *get* what we want from others or to *protect* ourselves from whatever hurt others can cause us. "So now I am giving you a new commandment: Love each other. *Just as I have loved you*, you should love each other" (John 13:34).

The bar is set high. Our aim must never be lower. Most people will never see the larger story God is telling unless Christians make that story visible by how we relate to each other. We're too easily satisfied with congenial relating, perhaps not even envisioning what it would mean to connect soul-to-soul with other travelers on the narrow road. If we know little of love's power in our Christian communities, we will release little of love's power by doing good in the world. We must learn to tell God's story by how we cooperate with the Spirit's deep work in each other's lives.

Now, it's obvious we cannot tell a story we do not know, unless of course the plot of the story comes naturally to us. The plot of Satan's story—self-centeredness—does. The plot of God's story—a better love—does not. We join God's story when we receive forgiveness for our relational sin and, at the same time, are given a nature that, like God's, is relationally holy. But then, as followers of Jesus, we need to learn the story God wants to tell through us, and we need to study its script.

The answers to the first six questions of spiritual theology unfold the story's plot and write the script. The seventh question asks how we cooperate with the Spirit's work. But only as we continually remember and digest the answers to the first six questions will we be able to discover the answer to the seventh. A brief review seems in order.

Question 1: *Who is God?* God is a relational being, a three-Person divine community. He is a *party happening*, an infinitely happy party.

Question 2: *What is God up to?* God is displaying the glory of divine love by inviting us to join His party, to learn to dance with the Trinity, to relate with others in rhythm with His relational nature.

Question 3: *Who are we?* We are little icons, images of the relational God created to reveal His hidden story of love by how we love, by putting the relational nature of Jesus on display.

202

Question 4: *What's gone wrong?* We left the party. We're now dancing in rhythm with the devil's story, thinking that looking out for ourselves first and foremost is necessary if we're to find happiness and avoid disappointment.

Question 5: *What has God done about our problem?* Jesus endured the death of isolation to which self-centeredness inevitably leads. We are now spared that consequence, forgiven for our sinful way of relating, made right with God, and made alive with the divine nature of other-centeredness, the nature the Holy Spirit placed within us and where He now lives.

Question 6: *How is the Spirit working to implement the divine solution to our human problem?* He continually exposes both the isolation we feel, brought on by self-centered relating, and the wickedness of relating with our immediately felt well-being first in our mind. In emptiness and brokenness we learn to pray the first thing prayer: Make me a little Christ! Why? Because when we feel desperately empty and helplessly broken, nothing matters more. We realize there is nothing better.

That's the larger story. And God is now trusting us to tell that story by relating in a new way, by battling for a kind of love that the Spirit's presence and power make possible. But how? That's the seventh question: *How can we cooperate with the Spirit's work?* Three words point us toward God's answer: *with, know,* and *give.*

God's Three-Part Answer to Question 7

With: Just Like Jesus

I will never leave you nor forsake you. (Heb. 13:5 ESV)

And be sure of this: I am with you always, even to the end of the age. (Matt. 28:20)

We cooperate with the Spirit's work in us and in those with whom we relate by never giving up on ourselves or others. I'm to be *with* you for the long haul and be present to you with confident hope that the vision for both of us to become little Christs is within reach, no matter what has happened to us or what we may have done.

A woman discovers that her husband has had multiple affairs. In tears, she tells him what she has learned. He becomes furious and hits her. She can be present to him with a vision for the godly man he could become by calling the police. What she does (and there are other options) matters less than *why* she does it. Her longing to be *with* him in a way that reveals her desire for him to gladly surrender to the love of Jesus can then be reflected in whatever interaction may follow.

No good friendship is without difficulties. Cooperating with the Spirit's work when tensions develop would include never abandoning the other to work through the tensions on their own. Even if we shake the dust off our feet and withdraw from someone, if we do so with their well-being in view, we would not abandon them in our prayers nor in our desire for reconciliation.

The battle for a better love is engaged when I surrender myself to tell God's story of *withness*, when I honor God's call to be present to another with an always sharpening vision of who the other could become as the Spirit continues His work.

Know: Just Like Jesus

O Lord, you have searched me and known me. (Ps. 139:1 ESV)

[God discerns] the thoughts and intentions of the heart. (Heb. 4:12 ESV)

God always knows. We don't. We come to *know* another when we see that person as a bearer of God's image, a little Christ in the making through an ongoing process that stirs our curiosity. And we know them as God does, never as fully of course, when our curiosity is guided by the wisdom the Bible provides about people. For example:

- As image-bearers, every person wants something, believes something, chooses something, and feels something.
- As bearers of God's relational image, every person most longs to be in satisfying relationship with another person.
- As fallen image-bearers, every person is driven by a core terror that in their mind justifies using others to get what they need and protecting themselves from what they fear.

The list goes on. Our wisdom deepens to the degree that we continue to explore the questions of spiritual theology. The answers provide ways of thinking about people, categories of understanding that can guide our curiosity with wisdom.

A friend tells you she is bored. Those who battle for a better love don't immediately pray for the bored woman. They don't quickly suggest something interesting for her to do. They don't glibly quote a Bible verse such as "[Don't] become weary and give up" (Heb. 12:3). Instead they listen, not passively but actively, with wisdom-guided curiosity. They ask questions about how her relationships are going, questions guided by the wisdom that living alive means living to love in relationships.

The battle for a better love is engaged when followers of Jesus reveal His story of love by wanting to *know* another person and gently but actively expressing curiosity about that person's soul. Guided by the wisdom revealed in the first six questions of spiritual theology, true disciples discern both their own struggle to relate well and the Spirit-provided avenue of movement toward relational holiness.

Give: Just Like Jesus

For just as the Father gives life to those he raises from the dead, so the Son gives life to anyone he wants. (John 5:21)

God is a giver who is always flowing outward, a relational God who delights in pouring His life into others. He created us in order to put His love on display, an incomprehensible love that moves with compassion toward persons whose nature it is to ignore Him, even to hate Him.

With perfect freedom, God releases all that He is to others. I must not do that. Unlike God, who I am includes a demand to get what I want from you before I will be open to give what you want from me. I must therefore reflect on my motives and potential impact on another before I give. God need not ask such questions as, *Am I wrongly looking out for myself? Because of insecurity, am I making a point to win respect? With careful calculation, am I giving only what puts me at little or no risk of rejection?* Those are questions you and I must ask, not God.

Reflection, if honest, will reliably provide reason for repentance. "God, what I want to say to this person or do for this person bears little resemblance to Your better love." It is repentance, involved in nearly every conversational encounter, that releases the life of God from my Spirit-indwelt nature, that frees me to offer a love that resembles the love of Jesus.

I *give* what is good through my words and deeds as I reflect on my motivation for giving and repent of the self-centeredness that is exposed. It is then that the love of Jesus trickles out of my redeemed heart into another. Sometimes it flows.

Satan, of course, offers counsel on how to relate well to others that appeals to us but interferes with the Spirit's movement, in both our lives and the lives of others.

Satan's Three-Part Answer to Question 7, Disguised as God's

Withdraw: Not Like Jesus

Has someone demeaned you, disappointed you, hurt you deeply? Back away. You don't deserve to be treated like that. Write them off as people unworthy of your friendship or love. Look after yourself. How will you be any good to anyone if you allow yourself in even a limited way to be with someone who tears you down? God loves you. You're worthy of similar love from others.

Overlook: Not Like Jesus

Never devote your strongest energy to knowing another person. See to it that *you* are known, but only to the degree that you want to be known, a degree that isn't too vulnerable. Play it safe. And it's better not to probe too deeply into someone else's life. You might discover things that upset or irritate you. But stay friendly. Interact meaningfully only with people you enjoy. God wants you to be happy. Overlook what's happening in others. Exploring people too deeply will only burden you. It might confuse you and make you feel inadequate. See obvious needs and do what you can to help. God expects nothing more.

Protect: Not Like Jesus

God will be with you to encourage you. But you must protect yourself from the harm others can inflict on you. Certainly you wouldn't walk through a deserted park late at night. It's too dangerous. So why would you open yourself in a relationship where you might get hurt? You need to feel good about yourself in order to make a good difference in this world. Only then will you experience the abundant life of enjoying yourself and doing good for others. Remember: your goal in every relationship is to enjoy who you are as someone worthy of being treated well. Never forget that God wants you happy. How could you be happy remaining in relationship with someone who treats you poorly? Extend love only to those whom you enjoy because they love you well.

Satan does all that he can to keep us preoccupied with second thing happiness, the happiness that comes when life and others treat us well. We need to hear God's story that leads us on the narrow road to first thing happiness, to the joy of putting Jesus on display even when life is difficult and others treat us poorly. We display Him best and cooperate with His Spirit's movement when we remain *with* others, seek to *know* them, and *give* to them the love Jesus freely gave to us.

PART 3

A Beautiful Story Is Unfolding, Even in the Darkest Night

Can you see the beauty of the story I am telling?

A little, yes. But only in glimpses too dim to consistently shine through me in how I relate.

You're still caught up in your smaller story. You're managing your life to bring about second things. And the pleasure you feel when life goes your way keeps you from longing to see the beauty of My story.

But Jesus, I do want to see the larger story of Your self-sacrificing love. I want to tell Your story by how I relate to others. But too often I fail, sometimes badly.

You always fall short of the way I love. But failure, when recognized and confessed, is your opportunity to rest in the hope of My forgiving, empowering love. Gaze on My cross. Celebrate My resurrection.

I think I've only been sipping the living water of Your love. Will I ever drink so freely and fully that Your kind of love will reliably flow out of me into others?

Keep walking the narrow road. My purposes for you will not fail.

20

Engage the Battle

We don't take him seriously. Before Jesus came, we had not seen
God, and we had not seen man either. We thought we knew
man, but utter humanity, breathed by the mouth of God . . .
we see that in Jesus.

Father Peregrine[1]

Is anything in life more important or more meaningfully sustaining and satisfying than knowing the relational God so well that
we live to make Him known by how we relate?

For most of us, the answer is, well, yes. Other things do matter
more. I'm writing this chapter two days after a US national election.
The winners are as excited as groupies at a rock concert. The losers
are already plotting for success in two years' time.

Love like Jesus? Of course that's a good thing, but getting our
country on the road to prosperity is what really matters. And aren't

we already loving like Him by working to better align our government policies with His principles?

After reviewing my history of cancer treatment and checking recent blood test results, at 1:35 p.m. yesterday my surgeon smiled and told me I was doing quite well. I noted the exact time when I heard the good news. In that moment I was more grateful for decent health than for an opportunity to love someone.

How quickly second things jump into first place. Perhaps they were already there. It's our health that's in question, not how we relate. We treat most people rather well. Our dieting and exercise habits require more disciplined attention than our relational efforts. Or so we think.

And I need to complete this book. The deadline is approaching. I signed a contract to deliver a manuscript to my editor, not to love him. That matters too, of course. But at least for now, turning in a marketable manuscript matters more. Doesn't it?

We had a new tankless water heater installed in our house six weeks ago. And now it's leaking. One more phone call to make. One more afternoon to wait for the plumber to come. Am I to love him when he arrives? I'm only hoping to keep my impatience in check. The leak needs fixing. There's always something that demands our time and attention and effort more than worrying about our relational formation.

And yet God's relational Holy Spirit keeps nudging us to ask ourselves how well we're relating to whoever comes across our path and inviting us to know His power to love like Jesus. But we don't have the energy to think about that. We brush aside the Spirit's question by reminding ourselves that we generally relate rather well, certainly better than how we're often treated by others.

I began this book by suggesting that nothing in today's culture, whether secular or religious, is less well understood or more wrongly undervalued than love—love as God lives it. Jesus puts on billboard display a kind of love that makes no sense to how we naturally think.

He unveiled love "above the sun," love that is willing to sacrifice what we think we need to be happy as we live "under the sun." (More on those two phrases in both the next and the final chapter.)

His way of relating brought on the kind of suffering we live to most avoid: rejection, criticism, betrayal, abandonment, slavery, and cruelty. He experienced it all and never stopped loving. If second thing happiness is our goal, loving like Jesus is not such a good idea.

We have a better plan: do good to others whom we can count on to do good to us. Arrange for and protect our sense of well-being. Only then, when we feel good about ourselves and our lives, will we move toward others with their well-being in mind.

We fall short of the relational beauty of God. We splash about in the muddy swamp of entitled expectations of others—I *need* this from him! I must *avoid* that from her!—when God has made a way for us to swim in the choppy but clear ocean of His dangerous love, gratefully distancing ourselves from the still-appealing shore of self-centeredness as we swim toward the harbor of relational formation.

As I near the end of this book, I'm still asking myself—am I in the battle? Am I swimming in the right direction? Or, to change metaphors, shouldn't I be farther along on the narrow road? Have I engaged the struggle for a better love? Does something else matter more to me? Am I content with how I relate to others, satisfied enough with how well I love to devote priority attention to more pressing matters, to fixing the leak in my water heater or feeling better about myself or electing a president who supports my values?

With all that's wrong and worrisome in our lives and in our world, is it really true that nothing matters more than knowing God well enough to be stunned by the beauty of divine love, and to therefore engage the most important battle that anyone in this life will ever fight, the battle for a better love? Listen to Paul express one of his best-known and least-embraced divinely authorized beliefs:

If I could speak all the languages of earth and of angels, *but didn't love others*, I would only be a noisy gong or a clanging cymbal. If I had the gift of prophecy, and if I understood all of God's secret plans and possessed all knowledge, and if I had such faith that I could move mountains, *but didn't love others*, I would be nothing. If I gave everything I have to the poor and even sacrificed my body, I could boast about it; *but if I didn't love others*, I would have gained nothing. (1 Cor. 13:1–3)

Do we believe Paul? If I could speak multiple languages, if I had an inside track to knowing God's secret plan and knew all there is to know, if my faith empowered me to perform dramatic miracles, if my concern for the poor made Mother Teresa look selfish, and if I sacrificed my physical comfort for a great cause but didn't love anyone the way Jesus loves, would my life really be worth nothing?

Paul knew Jesus. He knew what it meant to love others the way Jesus loves. Christians today, at least some, have the idea that to love like Jesus means to be nice to people, not rude or judgmental but pleasantly agreeable and cordially helpful. But Jesus was no tame kitten, no tail-wagging puppy. He gently but quite directly rebuked His good friend Martha (see Luke 10:41–42) and scathingly upbraided the Pharisees, calling them "blind guides" and "blind fools" (Matt. 23:16–17). He once turned to Peter, an ardent disciple, and said, "Get away from me, Satan!" (16:23). Hours before His crucifixion, Jesus first refused to answer the high priest's haughty question at His trial but then, when asked a second time, He enraged the scornful high priest with His answer (see Matt. 26:62–64).

What does it mean to love like that? When it served His Father's purpose, Jesus could be an apparently unassertive lamb ("He was led like a lamb to the slaughter" [Isa. 53:7]) or a roaring lion (to proud Jews, "For you are the children of your father the devil, and you love to do the evil things he does" [John 8:44]). In every relational encounter, He displayed the profoundly holy nature of divine love. No, Jesus was not nice, certainly not as most of us understand the term. We need to do some hard thinking to know what it means to reveal His nature in our interactions. We're not to relate as passive pushovers. But neither are we to indulge our urge to push over anyone who gets in the way of our enjoyment of second things.

A good friend (or perhaps a spouse or child) treats you badly. That person believes his unkind behavior toward you is justified because you first failed him. You don't agree, but you express your willingness to work through the tension in your relationship. He angrily declares the friendship is over. You want to battle for a better love. What would that mean?

Satan has a few suggestions, and they have their appeal. Here's one: hold your ground. Realize your friend is immature and back away until he grows up. Here's another: apologize for a wrong you don't believe you committed. Keep the peace. Do whatever you can to restore the relationship on his terms. If you are strong-minded, you'll likely prefer the first suggestion. Only weak people would opt for the second.

You know you've traveled some distance on the narrow road when you realize it's the devil's voice tempting you to look out for yourself, not to advance God's glory by how you relate. You want to hear the Spirit's voice. You listen. You read. You pray. But no direct instruction comes, no specific steps are outlined.

Maybe backing away from an angry friend would be a way of loving him, giving him unpressured time to cool off. Or acknowledging that perhaps you had failed him, though you do not see it, might reflect the energy of love. You don't know. *You are now engaged in the difficult, sometimes confusing battle for a better love.* The battle would be easier if you knew exactly what to do. You long to tell God's story but you don't know the lines you're to recite. Perhaps there are no scripted lines. *Perhaps the Spirit works in another way.*

Consider this: when your mind and heart are open to however the Spirit of holy love might lead, when you understand that divine love sacrifices pride for the sake of another's well-being, when you deliberately envision who your troublesome friend could become if he yielded to the call of God, then your Spirit-saturated soul will release something of Jesus through whatever you choose to do.

It's God's work in your soul that releases something good in the way you move toward the soul of another. And remember this: *success in the battle for a better love must not be finally measured by the visible impact you make on another*. If you make it your goal to see the fruit of your loving efforts, you will feel pressure to get it right. But desire a humbled friend and a restored relationship and you will pray, demanding nothing, entitled to nothing, but praying for a much-desired second thing blessing. Make it your goal to delight the Father by honoring Christ however you choose to relate and you will know joy in the middle of ongoing sorrow over a broken, perhaps never-to-be-repaired relationship.

The narrow road to life is narrow. It's only on the broad road that you will perhaps successfully scramble to find formulas for achievement in arranging for second things, steps to carry you to second thing happiness. On the narrow road you might strongly rebuke your friend, like Jesus sometimes rebuked His friends; you might offer to share what is happening in you, as Jesus did with His three closest friends in Gethsemane; or you might shake the dust from a difficult relationship off your feet as you move on with your life, as Jesus once told His disciples to do. *A surrendered will to love like Jesus releases the passion of the loving Jesus*. You might later realize a different course of action would have released more of His passion. That Spirit-granted wisdom would then enable you to move farther along on the narrow road with greater discernment.

As you keep walking the narrow road, engage the battle for a better love by asking yourself, and honestly answering before God, several questions:

- Do I sincerely long for God to work in the one who has hurt me so badly?
- Can I envision who my friend could become and pray for that vision to be realized?
- Am I open to however the Spirit might lead me to respond in this difficult circumstance?
- Have I asked God to search my heart to point out anything in my attitude that offends Him?
- Will I make known my sadness and struggle to godly friends and seek their wisdom?

You may receive direct leading from the Lord on what to do, or you may not. Either way, if you are asking these questions (and others like them) and are decisively open to answering them honestly, you are engaged in the battle for a better love. You are not living *under the sun*, where you would be determined to make the best of a bad situation but are now living *above the sun*, eager to know how the story of your life can best tell the story of God.

Is there one central question we must ask in order to hear God's answer, the answer that will guide us as we walk through life on the narrow road? In the next chapter, I make clear the question I wrote this book to answer.

The final chapter then explores what it means to live *under the sun*, where telling Satan's story leads us into the quicksand of a wasted life, and calls us to live where we belong, *above the sun*, where telling God's story carries us into the joy of indulging our deepest desire: to put Jesus on display in all our relationships.

21

The Answer

To What Question?

There is nothing more boring than an answer to a question you care nothing about.

Peter Kreeft[1]

Among a dozen others, two possible mistakes in the writing of this book stand out to me as mistakes I really don't want to make. One is this: I don't want to provide a book-length answer to a question no one is asking. The second is related: I don't want to offer a long-winded, abstruse answer to an important question all of us should be asking, an answer that will prove to be more confusing than clarifying.

If the previous chapters haven't already done so, I want these final two chapters to make plain the question I'm venturing to articulate and to arouse urgent interest in finding its answer. With equal passion, I hope that what I'm about to say will spur you to thoughtfully and seriously consider the answer I'm presenting to an important question. That question, however, is sometimes difficult to ask. Let me illustrate.

Without warning, a pastor friend was dismissed by his church elders. No explanation was given beyond, "We don't believe you're the person to lead our church to the next level." The man was confused and bitter. And scared. With a wife, four kids, and a mortgage, he needed a job. You can guess what question was uppermost in his mind, the same one I would be asking if I were in his situation: *What am I supposed to do now?* Should he be asking a different question, more urgently but calmly asked? Could he? Could I?

A middle-aged woman had been married for ten years to her second husband and was disappointed—again. Her first husband was an unrepentant sex addict. This one was moral, kind to a fault, and weak. When conflict arose between them, always in his mind precipitated by her, he would smile and hide. "What am I supposed to do?" she asked me. "I feel alone, angry, and depressed. I just can't respect him. I can't bear the thought of living one more year with this man." Is she asking the question God most wants to answer? Does her question evidence any real interest in the story God is telling?

Another friend was discouraged. Neither his marriage nor his work were going well. "I've always been pretty self-confident. Now I feel like a loser. My self-esteem is dragging on the ground. What am I supposed to do to feel good about myself and my life again?" Until he raises a different question, a more important one, this book will mean nothing to him. Nor will the gospel.

A woman's teenage daughter was recently date-raped by her Christian boyfriend. The girl retreated into a dark place. Mood-altering medication helped a little. But she won't go for counseling. "Why should I?" she said. "My life is ruined." Her mother is fighting a battle on three fronts, and a fourth lingers in her mind.

- She hates this boy. She knows she is supposed to forgive him. That's what Christians should do.
- She doesn't know how best to help lift her daughter's depression. Neither her pastor nor the counselor she consulted provided clear direction.
- She is furious with her husband for remaining awkwardly distant from their daughter. When she tells him how mad she is, he backs away further.

The fourth battlefront exists because she is a Christian. She asks herself: *Where is God in all of this? Why did He allow this? How am I supposed to handle this mess?*

Understandably, she is angry, worried, and confused. But only when a different question rises up from a deeper place within her, where the Holy Spirit lives, will she be open to hearing what God is up to in the middle of the mess and to cooperating with His eternal purposes as she relates with her daughter and husband and thinks about her attitude toward the abusive boyfriend.

When I taught counseling at a seminary, more than once I overheard disgruntled students complaining as they left a lecture on some fine point of theology. "Does that professor have a life outside his classroom? He's answering questions that no one in the real world is asking. Does he really expect us to someday stand behind a pulpit and bore everyone to death with teaching that has nothing to do with their lives?"

Perhaps those students' upcoming job is mine now, to arouse interest in the questions God has answered, questions profoundly relevant to everyone's life and to everyone's ill-fated pursuit of happiness. In this book, I don't want to distance myself from real life and talk only about abstract theology. That would be mistake number one. Mistake number two follows on its heels: I don't want to arouse compelling interest in an important question God answers and then provide an answer that fails to speak clearly and meaningfully, with soul-changing power.

Perhaps you remember. Years ago, on the late-night talk show he hosted, Johnny Carson would don a swami's hat, lift a sealed envelope to his ear, pause two seconds, then solemnly announce, "The answer is . . ." He would then open the envelope, remove the note inside, and read the question he had just claimed to answer. The humor was in the obvious mismatch between the question and the answer.

Just last week, I stumbled onto a television rerun of "Carson Classics." When I saw the "answer first/question later" sketch, I wondered: Is there a not-so-funny mismatch between the answer I'm providing in this book and the question we should all be asking? Will my answer ring true to sincere disciples of Jesus who are asking the crucial question that life requires we ask?

You've just read twenty chapters. With some fearful hesitation, let me now, in two sentences, summarize the answer I'm giving in this book to perhaps the most important question anyone could ask:

> If you are walking through life on the narrow road, you are living your life in the larger story. If you are living your life in the larger story, you are engaged in the battle for a better love because you are looking at life from above the sun, not from under the sun.

That's the answer. But what's the question? Before I respond to *that* question, let me direct your attention to the four key phrases in these two sentences. The first three have already been thought about in earlier chapters and need only brief review. The fourth was passingly mentioned in chapter 20 and requires discussion, which will be the topic of the next chapter. Better understanding of the answer contained in those two sentences and four key phrases might help to clarify the question they refer to.

Phrase 1: walking through life on the narrow road

Phrase 2: living your life in the larger story

Phrase 3: engaging the battle for a better love

Phrase 4: looking at life from above the sun, not from under the sun

Walking through Life on the Narrow Road

It is wrong to assume you are on the narrow road simply because your life is hard. Life is hard for everyone—atheists and Christians, luke-warm followers of Jesus and true disciples alike. Hardship does not define the narrow road; it presents an opportunity for Christians to take the next step on the narrow road with fresh resolve and firm hope. And you must not think you are on the narrow road because you live a moral life, doing your best to do the Christian dos and to not do the Christian don'ts. If that is your understanding of what it means to walk through life on the narrow road, a Pharisee would be a suitable guide.

You *are* on the narrow road if you are keenly aware that two stories are being told in every minute of every day, one by Satan and one by God. Travelers on the narrow road sense the appeal of both stories, too often with a stronger attraction to the wrong one. But they prayerfully discern which story is which and to what end each story is leading. As the Holy Spirit works, they get wind of the stench of Satan's relationship-deadening but attractively disguised story and they catch the fragrance of God's relationship-building and attractively demanding story. And they increasingly come to understand what it means to tell the story their redeemed hearts most long to tell by how they relate.

Living Your Life in the Larger Story

You are living your life in the larger story of God if you long to know everything that has been revealed in the Bible about His story so that you can follow its relational script. If instead you settle for only a statement of what you believe to be Christian truth and an awareness of a few biblical principles you try to follow, you are living in a smaller, non-relational story.

Storytellers, tellers of the larger story, like to imagine how the story began in eternity past, before time began, when there was only God, three divine Persons enjoying a community of love. These storytellers then fast-forward through eternal ages to the dramatic moment when time began. God's storytellers know that God created them for one supreme purpose, to see in Jesus and then to display a kind of love that loves the unlovable, the rebel, the fool, the proudly independent, and the pleasure-obsessed hedonist—a love willing to personally experience whatever suffering is needed to transform little devils into little Christs, and the only kind worthy to be called love.

If you and I are among those who are living life in God's larger story, we are eagerly anticipating the day when time will end, when every slowly forming little Christ will suddenly be fully formed and welcomed into the divine community to enjoy divine happiness in a world made new by holy divine power. Between eternity past and eternity future, God's storytellers, hopefully including you and me, seize the opportunity that time provides to display the surprising love of Jesus to a watching world, even when we unfairly lose our job or struggle in an unhappy marriage or suffer a severe blow to our self-confidence or wrestle in anguish with a family disaster. We know we are living life in the larger story when we see its plot, grasp it with hope, and long to advance the storyline by the way we relate.

Engaging the Battle for a Better Love

True disciples of Jesus battle for a better love, His kind of love; they don't centrally battle for a better life of happy circumstances. Battle for a better life and you will not battle for a better love. Battle for a better love and you discover a better life as God defines it and as

Jesus experienced it, along with happy circumstances as God chooses to provide them.

You are most fully engaged in the battle when you recognize the danger it invites and realize, perhaps to your surprise, that like Jesus you're willing to risk the worst. You will then become more acutely aware that you are a double being. Those who battle to love like Jesus are tempted to leave the battlefield, to protect their hearts from further disappointment and hurt, to wreak revenge on a spouse or friend who harmed them. In those seasons of temptation, Christians who long to love like Jesus hear the Spirit's call to pour grace onto people they have good reason not to like. The call will seem unreasonable, even foolish, as if it's asking too much and is perhaps a call beyond their capability to answer.

It is then that those of us who are engaged in the good fight will understand that *we* are the battlefield. We resolve to be good soldiers of Jesus, but sometimes we switch sides and fight for His enemy, and ours. But then we confess our relational sin of living as an individual self and not as a relational soul and worshipfully rest in God's amazing grace. When we do put Jesus on display, especially in a difficult relationship, we sing praises to the divine community, to each Person for His part in making it possible. We come to more deeply realize that we do love the story of God and the God who calls us into a good battle that one day will be eternally won.

Walking through life on the narrow road, living life in the larger story of God, engaging the battle for a better love: that is what is involved in following Jesus as a true disciple who daily counts the cost.

And that is what I believe is God's answer to the question that every honest person will ask as they live their lives in this uncertain, unsatisfying, and unhappy world, always longing to rest in the exciting climax of God's good story, to experience the soul satisfaction we were created to enjoy, to celebrate living loved and living to love in a world without thorns or tears, *to see Jesus and be with Him forever.* Most people, however, find a broad road to travel on through life

224

that lets them deny how uncontrollably uncertain, how inevitably unsatisfying, and how acutely unhappy life is, a road that both frees them to never ask the one big question that only God can answer and empowers them to laugh in derision at the morbid folks who ask it.

You've heard my answer. What is the question? There are many ways to ask it, but every version boils down to this:

> How can I make sense out of life as I experience it? Is there one story that brings everything that happens into line with one great purpose, a purpose I will find meaningful and be able to believe is good and worth all the trouble I cannot explain?

Look at life under the sun and you will see no story that weaves everything that happens into one grand and glorious purpose. Every religious story told under the sun, including a "Christian" version, is simply a disguised version of the story Satan wants told. Every secular story told under the sun, whether in politics or in universities, encourages people to believe they can change themselves and the world without depending on resources available only in Jesus Christ and the good news He brought to earth.

In the final chapter, we will explore how looking at life from under the sun makes a life lived for God impossible. And we will consider what it means to look at life from above the sun and to see the story that is unseen from under the sun, the story that brings everything into line with one great purpose that no one, not even the devil, can thwart.

22

Life

Above and Under the Sun

If our view of life goes no further than "under the sun," all our endeavors will have an undertone of misery.

Michael A. Eaton[1]

It is one thing to believe in God as a supporting actor in the drama of our story, a story that begins at our birth and ends at our death. It is quite another to know ourselves to be small but significant actors in the eternal drama of God's story, a story that begins in eternity past, stretches out from Genesis 1:1 through Revelation 22:21, and continues as a dance of love into eternity future.

Under the sun is

- everything that can be experienced through our five senses and understood by human reason.
- everything that shapes the smaller story of our lives.

Above the sun is

- everything that can be seen only with Spirit-granted faith and known only through divine revelation.
- everything that shapes the larger story of God.

I'm struggling. Some struggles are brought on by what happens to us. This one is not. I'm bringing it on myself.

Something's not right. As I begin writing this final chapter, the idea of taking further steps on the narrow road feels more like an unwelcome burden than a hope-filled opportunity. Recognizing and resisting Satan's story by continuing to tell God's story seems, right now, like annoyingly hard work with only long-delayed results. The faith required to live His larger story is a little wobbly.

There's something else too. The hassle of dealing with an unexpected challenge that I'm now facing is draining both my motivation and energy to keep battling to love well, like Jesus. For now, a few miles on a broad road, an easier and more pleasant one, seems appealing.

About three weeks ago, before I got word of this latest challenge, I sensed what I believed then and believe now was the gentle nudge of heaven's Spiritual Director to read Ecclesiastes. I didn't know why. I think I do now. He wanted to speak to me through the only book in the Bible where a man struggling to make sense of his life hears nothing from God and sees no visible, feel-able evidence of His involvement. (The struggling man was either Solomon or perhaps a sage who reported Solomon's thinking. We can't be certain who actually wrote Ecclesiastes. For ease of communication, I'll refer to Solomon as the writer.)

Solomon, who had everything life in this world can offer, looked at life without considering that a larger story was being told, blocking any hope of joy in knowing that a story beyond what he could see was under way. Solomon reported that he saw only what human sense could observe and understood only what human reason could fathom. *He was a man living under the sun.*

Michael A. Eaton spotted what I believe may be the single most important message of the book, a message that my divine Spiritual Director wants me, and I suspect all of us, to hear. For good reason: *failure to hear this message destines us to a wasted life.* The quote from his book that captures the message of Ecclesiastes headlines this chapter. Let me rephrase it a bit here:

> People who look at life from under the sun will sense an undertone of misery in all their seemingly laudable efforts to change the world and to make their own lives meaningful and satisfying.

An undertone of misery. That poignant phrase puts words to the heart of my struggle. I feel detached from what I know to be true, unmoved by what should excite my heart. If Eaton is correct, and I think he is, then I must ask myself a sober question: Am I, like Solomon, looking at life from under the sun? Am I living on the surface of life, discounting what my faith tells me is true and dismissing what God has revealed to me in the Bible?

Could it be that many declared followers of Jesus are viewing life from under the sun without knowing it, without realizing what we're doing? Are we living shallow lives, thinking we're quite serious about our Christianity but wondering why, beneath our breezy pleasantness, we sometimes sense an undertone of misery? We must be clear. True disciples of Christ do groan inwardly, but in hope, not in misery. Feeling a throbbing ache in our souls that reminds us we're not yet home is a mark of maturity, not superficiality. God has taken us "to the high places of blessing in him. Long before he laid down the earth's foundations, he had us in mind, had settled on us as the focus of his love, to be made whole and holy by his love" (Eph. 1:3–4 MSG). That's reason for joy, not misery. But until we're home, the ache remains, a hopeful grieving that is different from the undertone of misery.

Recently, however, I think I've been experiencing murmuring misery more than optimistic lament. I therefore must wonder if the story my life is telling by how I think and relate is, at least for the moment, shaped more by what I see than by what God has revealed.

Most of us arrange for enough distraction and denial to mute the whispering voice of meaninglessness. We write off the undertone of misery as nothing more than a bad mood and wait for it to pass. We keep responsibly busy with the everyday demands of life. We do good and helpful deeds for people in need. And we indulge appropriate pleasures such as eating good food, socializing with good friends, or going to a good movie.

As Christians we take God's principles seriously and live by them as best we can. Too many of us see little need to explore the inside world of our souls. Navel-gazing is for melancholics. It is better to forget childhood hurts and manage current disappointments. Counseling and spiritual direction are always available if needed, just like surgery. And then something happens.

Several days ago an email arrived from my doctor. Blood test results indicate I am now facing a fourth battle with cancer. The first two, one nearly two decades ago and the second three years ago, were both successfully resolved with major surgery. My third battle, the one I mentioned earlier in this book, was treated eight months ago with a less invasive procedure. Things looked good. But now, more scans and further treatment seem inevitable. I hear the undertone of misery. The story I had in mind is off-script.

In this moment, as I'm sitting at my desk writing these words and sipping yet another cup of coffee, I feel less inclined than I did a week ago to battle for a better love—less inclined to live the larger story and less inclined to stay on the narrow road. But reading Ecclesiastes has brought something into clear focus that might otherwise have remained fuzzy. It's this: *I cannot blame the return of cancer for my weakened desire to follow Jesus.* The cause lies in me, in my soul, not in my body.

I am looking at life from under the sun, feeling somewhat entitled to my smaller story going well, willing to walk the narrow road as long as God remains reasonably cooperative with my plans and dreams for life. My smaller story is off-script. And this undertone of misery has become God's megaphone to let me know that my gaze is not fixed on the larger story.

A caring friend just received word that my cancer is back. She responded with passion, "Oh, Larry, I'm so sorry. I think Satan is out to stop you from doing all the good you do that is helping so many people. I'm going to pray really hard that he won't get his way, that your cancer will be fully healed and you'll be able to continue your ministry with even more energy."

I appreciate her concern, and I value her prayers. Both are warmly intended and good. I hope God grants her request. He might. Or He might not. Having spent time in Ecclesiastes, I realize I would appreciate even more a sensitive and discerning concern that something in my soul needs priority attention. I might be elevating restored health and continued ministry, both second things, to first thing status. In God's story, that is far more off-script than another bout with cancer.

A glimpse of life from above the sun, always available in Scripture and prayer, lets me see that the purpose of life as told in God's story is not to stay alive but to bring God glory while we live. Jesus followers do that best when we redeem whatever time God gives us to live in this world by displaying the love of Jesus in all that we do, especially in how we relate. *That* is kingdom living. *That* is bringing God's relational kingdom to earth. *That* is our highest calling.

My biggest challenge is not cancer. Of course God wants me to do all I can to rally my body back to health. It is, after all, where His Spirit has taken up residence. But my biggest challenge that requires the deepest work of the Spirit is for me to view life from above the sun even as I continue living my life under the sun in a world where cancer sometimes comes without explanation. God has made available to me the faith to know with certainty that through good times and bad His story is on track, even when bad times get worse. The first thing, the work He has already begun to form me into a little Christ, will continue until it is finally finished when Christ returns. The story of God, invisible from under the sun, is reliably unfolding through all that comes my way as I live under the sun. That truth defines *providence*.

I long to be a man of faith. I want to rest in the assurance that God is always up to something good. My next step on the narrow road is not to quiet the undertone of misery but to feel its intensity so strongly that I passionately ask the question I'm writing this book to answer:

> God, how can I make sense out of life as I experience it? Are You really telling a good story, a story that brings everything I see and feel into line with a loving purpose, a purpose that if I saw I'd thirst to honor, a purpose that is worth all the pain and fear that I can neither explain nor manage?

In His answer to the Seven Questions of Spiritual Theology, God has revealed the love story He is right now telling to me and to you, and to anyone who is listening.

I exist. I have always existed as a three-Person community of love (Q1). My heart of love longs to include others in My party, to share in My happiness (Q2). I therefore created you in My image and likeness as a relational person, capable of receiving My love with joy and with joy pouring it into others (Q3).

But you refused to trust My love. You set out on a foolish, ill-fated course to get from others what only I can provide. That road leads to the misery of living unloved and unable to love. And as you taste that misery along the way, you demand relief by protecting yourself from others rather than giving yourself to others. And you seek pleasure in second things, mistaking the happiness they bring for a better, different kind of happiness, first thing happiness, the happiness I created you to enjoy. That journey ends in relational isolation, the misery that comes when you live apart from Me, the only source of real love and true happiness (Q4).

Real love, the love that defines who I am, is committed to your well-being at any cost to Myself. I therefore suffered the consequence of your lack of love, your rebellion against Me that left you ruled by the passion of self-centeredness. The cross has you covered. You are now forgiven, restored into relationship with Me, and made a participant in My divine nature (Q5). I am now alive in you, empowering you to seize the opportunity to experience Me by expressing Me to others. But it is an opportunity you will not meaningfully seize until you feel how miserable you are when you continue to live for second things and how broken you should be over your recognized relational sin. Only then will you value My love as your supreme good (Q6).

Tell My story by living together with other true disciples, living with each other, living to know each other, and living to give My life to each other. Make visible to everyone who knows you what you can see when you view life from above the sun (Q7).

Paul, perhaps more than any true disciple since, clearly heard God's story and lived to tell it. Listen to his testimony, with a few clarifying comments added.

I once thought these things [*prestige, power, and privilege*] were valuable, but now I consider them worthless because of what Christ has done. Yes, everything else [*every source of meaning and happiness available under the sun*] is worthless when compared with [*the first thing*] the infinite value of knowing Christ Jesus my Lord. For his sake I have discarded everything else [*everything I once believed brought life*], counting it all as garbage [*the Greek word translated* garbage *literally means what we flush down the toilet*] so that I could gain Christ and become one with him [*a follower of Christ who is being formed into a little Christ*]. (Phil. 3:7–9)

My struggle now is not to mute the undertone of misery but to see it mutate into the ache of thirsting to look at life from above the sun, to hear the story God is telling, and to yearn to know Christ and to make Him known.

My struggle to increasingly surrender to the Spirit's work as He forms Christ in me will continue until I see Jesus face-to-face. So will yours. But it's a good struggle. Fix your eyes of faith on the story unfolding above the sun, the love story revealed in the sixty-six love letters God has written to us.

Walk the narrow road. Live the larger story. Battle for a better love. It's why we're alive.

Afterword

Let me offer a few suggestions for shifting your view of life from under the sun to above the sun. It's a journey worth taking.

1. Trace your history of relational disappointment, how others have failed you, from early days to now. Don't identify yourself as a victim. Rather, feel your deep desire that remains unsatisfied, the inconsolable longing that will never be fully satisfied until you are with Jesus. Face your emptiness. *Embrace your thirst.*

2. Reflect on your experience with fear. Explore the core terror that so often influences how you relate to others, not the fear of never being seen, or being seen and unwanted, but the core terror of being seen and unwanted *for good reason*. Realize your relational sin entitles you to being abandoned. *Embrace your brokenness.*

3. Face the disturbing fact that nothing is now as it should be, that something is wrong with everything. Acknowledge what history demonstrates, that the best efforts of scientists, politicians, philanthropists, ideologues, and religious leaders to remake the world into all we want it to be will fail. *Embrace futility.*

4. Agree with Solomon. He "discovered that God [had] dealt a tragic existence to the human race" (Eccles. 1:13). *Embrace misery.*

5. Respond to thirst, brokenness, futility, and misery by opening your heart and mind to God. He has spoken. The story He is telling is revealed in the Bible. It's a good story. *Embrace hope.*

6. See yourself at a crossroads. Either you will tell your smaller story of ongoing thirst, brokenness, futility, and misery that leads to nothingness, or you will tell God's larger story of anticipated fullness, promised restoration, enjoyed meaning, and experienced joy that fuels no stronger desire than to know and resemble the crucified God. *Embrace Christ.*

7. When you embrace Christ as His true disciple, prepare to walk a narrow road to the abundance of desire and power to be formed like Jesus. Commit to living the larger story that involves suffering now but ends in an eternal climax of joy, with delicious tastes now. Accept the call to battle for a better love, to enjoy the privilege of putting Jesus on display as you relate to others. *Embrace life, a different kind of happiness, an appetizing taste of what lies ahead.*

One Final Question

Was Jesus filled with God's Spirit as He hung on the cross, even during those three hours of darkness when He experienced His Father's abandonment?

The question is important. The answer has everything to do with whether it is possible for us today to know joy during especially difficult times and with how the Spirit releases in us the same joy that Jesus knew during His most difficult time.

Think of it this way. If Jesus was filled with the Spirit during the entire duration of His agony on the cross, and if He never quenched or grieved the Spirit (which of course He would never do), then He must have experienced the fruit of the Spirit's fullness in His worst moments. And, among other outgrowths, the Spirit's fruit includes joy.

If the Spirit remained alive in the man Jesus during those long hours on the cross, then the unbelievable becomes astonishingly believable: *Jesus knew joy while He suffered, and so can we.* We can know that there is a joy that survives and continues through the worst suffering we will ever experience.

The point bears repeating: if Jesus was indeed filled with God's Spirit as He suffered on the cross, it follows that He must have experienced the Spirit's fruit during that entire time. Because joy is the sweetness of the Spirit's fruit, Jesus—can we say it?—must have known joy even as He ached over the desertion of His friends, the betrayal of Peter, the cruelty of the soldiers, the mocking of spectators, the onslaught of the devil, and above all, the impossible-to-anticipate horror of the Father's abandonment sensed for the first and only time in all eternity.

I read what I have just written and wonder: *What does it mean to experience the happiness of Jesus whether I am enjoying delightful blessings or enduring devastating trials?* What must remain alive in you that only the Spirit can keep alive when a spouse rejects you, when a loved one dies, when a child breaks your heart, when disease threatens long-term disability or death, when unemployment and mounting bills terrify you?

By faith, am I to assume that a Christlike desire to love remains inextinguishable within the deepest regions of my Spirit-filled soul? Am I then to indulge that desire in whatever opportunity to love another presents itself? Will a vigorously deliberate choice to act on that desire release a flow of love pouring out of me? And will that flow somehow, mysteriously, be accompanied by a realized destiny that I will rightly know as joy?

To each of those questions, I respond with a yet-to-be-fully-tested *yes.* But if Jesus was not filled with the Spirit during the crucifixion, my cautious yes becomes a sad *no.* I then would have more reason to doubt that, in the worst of times, the Spirit can generate joy. We need an answer: *Was He or was He not a Spirit-filled man as He suffered on the cross?*

As I think my way through that question, let me begin with an assumption. From the moment Jesus was conceived, the Holy Spirit, who was alone responsible for the conception in the virgin Mary, was pleased to take up immediate residence in the only human ever conceived as a holy unborn person.

After twelve years of sinless living, can anyone doubt that the indwelling Spirit inspired Jesus when, as a preteen, He amazed scholarly Jewish teachers with His understanding of spiritual things as He talked with them in the temple?

Then, at age thirty, Jesus was baptized by John. In the moment He was lifted from the water, Jesus was praying. Only Luke supplies that detail. And the Greek word translated *praying* means to "wish forward," most likely referring to our Lord's determination to move toward His death. As Jesus was praying, the always present and indwelling Spirit met Him in a new way. In the form of a dove, God's Spirit descended on Jesus to *anoint* Him, to call and equip Him with divine passion to accomplish the purpose for which the Father had sent Him: to live, die, and be resurrected as a perfectly Spirit-led human, an unblemished lamb sacrificed for the sins of the world.

Fast-forward three years. Jesus was now in Gethsemane, overcome by what He knew awaited Him. An angel appeared to strengthen Jesus when, as a deeply troubled man, He felt the collision of the anointing Spirit against His thoroughly innocent longing to avoid experiencing the unbearable physical pain of crucifixion and the never-before-experienced relational pain of becoming what both He and the Father abhorred. And Jesus never left the narrow road. Overcome more by God's call than by His terror, in the freedom of victory in the battle to love, He resolutely moved toward Calvary.

And then He was hanging on the cross. Between nine o'clock and noon on that Friday morning, before thick darkness covered the land from noon till three o'clock, Jesus uttered three cries that could only have come from a human heart filled with the very nature of God and surrendered to the Spirit's passion (see John 19:26–27; Luke 23:34, 43). Listen to them:

- "Father, forgive these sadistic soldiers who have just driven nails into my hands and feet."

- "Woman, look on John as your son. John, receive Mary as your mother."
- "Guilty thief, today you will be with me in an eternal paradise of joy."

And then the darkness came. At its narrowest, Jesus kept walking the narrow road all the way to His death that brings us life. During those infinitely long three hours when Jesus had no sense of His Father's loving presence, when neither Father nor Son experienced the joyful intimacy both had known without a moment's interruption throughout eternity, when Satan was given full access to the soul of Jesus, *where was the Spirit*? Had the third Person of the Trinity separated Himself from the Son as the Father had done?

Consider the implications of how that question could be answered. As a human, fully God but still a flesh and blood person like you and me, was Jesus left to His own resources to endure, without shrinking back, the worst the devil could throw at Him, to suffer nothing less than the full experience of hell?

Or was the Spirit still present *in* Jesus as the indwelling Spirit and *on* Jesus as the anointing Spirit? I see no reason to doubt that the Spirit was present in Gethsemane when the Roman soldiers came to arrest Him. With quiet confidence beyond the capacity of a mere human, even a sinless one, Jesus told His disciples that one word to His Father and more than twelve legions of angels would immediately appear to rescue Him from the murderous intent of both Rome and the Jewish leaders. (It's worth a brief mention that a Roman legion consisted of six thousand soldiers. We sing, "He could have called ten thousand angels." More accurately, perhaps, we should sing, "He could have called more than 72,000 angels.")

Another question occurs to me. During those three hours of darkness *could* Jesus have appealed to His Father to send hordes of angels on a rescue mission? In the worst moment of His agony, fully committed to the work that only His continued suffering would accomplish, was Jesus somehow *unable* to call for divine help? And if He had asked His Father to immediately put an end to His misery, would His Father have *refused* the request?

On both counts, no! It is unimaginable. Jesus always had the choice to either remain on the cross or to be removed from it by angels. And I can only think that the Father would have honored either choice. But we're speaking of hypotheticals that love would not allow. Given each member of the Trinity's shared resolve of suffering love, this question is settled: Jesus would *not* fail to accomplish the Godhead's passionate determination to reveal the glory of divine love by saving sinners. Freely and purposefully, as a man on a mission, Jesus willingly chose to suffer the death sinners deserve so that with decisive authority He could say, "*It is finished.* The devil is conquered. Death is defeated. Sin has been punished. Intimate relationship with the Trinity is available to people who deserve eternal loneliness and eternal forsakenness by God. I have completed the work my Father sent me to do. His eternal love is now freely released in time, into everyone who knows their need of its power."

But here is another question: Was the choice Jesus made to endure the full suffering of the cross, including His Father's abandonment, enabled only by the strength of human commitment or also by the strength of the Spirit's fullness? The Father clearly had forsaken His Son. Had the Spirit left Him as well? If so, I cannot imagine for a moment that Jesus knew anything of joy as He endured those hours of horror. No human could.

But if, in a way beyond our understanding, Jesus was filled with the Spirit, then in His worst agony, as the Spirit's passion found expression in the Savior's words of love, the Spirit's unquenched fullness would be accompanied by joy, the Spirit's reliable fruit—not the tasty fruit of life's blessings but the satisfying fruit of ultimate resolve to reveal divine love. And we could then believe that the same joy Jesus knew could be ours in our worst moments—*if, in the Spirit's power, we loved like Jesus.* The measure of our joy would depend

241

on the measure of our love. The battle for a better love would then have strong appeal.

Had the Spirit departed from Jesus during those hours on the cross, including the three hours of darkness? My answer is no. For two reasons—both densely theological and therefore beyond my mind's ability to fully grasp, let alone fully explain—I believe that Jesus, in some way that is mysteriously thrilling to my heart, was filled with God's Spirit in every moment of His life and in every moment of His dying.

Reason 1

I understand the Spirit to be the eternally loving, fully personal reality of the relational bond between the Father and the Son, the expression of a relationship so transcendently beautiful that the spirit of that relationship is the eternal Person of the Holy Spirit, who with neither beginning nor end proceeds from the Father and the Son.

Imagine spending time with a couple married for sixty-plus years who are now more one than ever before. In their presence, you would feel the spirit of their unity. Now let your mind wonder at the eternal relationship of perfect love between the Father and the Son, a kind of love that would reveal the married couple's love to be only an incomplete facsimile. The spirit of the Father-Son relationship is so infinitely glorious and alive that *it*, the spirit, is *He*, a Person who is the divine nature of pure love, unblemished relationality, the Spirit of holy love.

Now imagine the unimaginable. Imagine the relationship between the Father and Son *entirely* severed. Would there then have been no relationship from which the Spirit could proceed? Would He then have ceased to exist? Unthinkable! Blasphemous! He is eternal. I therefore cannot imagine that the Father's abandonment of the Son was complete. Something remained of their union even during the

Father's abandonment of the Son and the Son's terrible agony of realized desertion. If that is true, then the Spirit of their union was still fully alive in that moment of abandonment and therefore available to be present to Jesus in His worst agony.

But what was it that remained of the Father-Son relationship during those three hours of the Father's abandonment and the Son's experience of forsakenness? And what continued to proceed from the divine Father and the divine Son that could fill the human Jesus with divine Spirit?

Reason 2

Grant that something remained in the relationship between the Father and Son, and one thrilling possibility comes to mind. Could it be it was their *relationship of enjoyed intimacy*, grounded in love, that was in fact completely dissolved for those three hours? And could it be that their *relationship of shared purpose*, equally grounded in love, remained intact? Fellowship in mutually enjoyed intimacy was broken. That much is clear. But perhaps the fellowship of mutual steadfast mission continued, a oneness rooted in the sacrificing, suffering love of divine resolve to pay whatever price was required to display the glory of a kind of love that could restore rebels against God into His family. The union of a kind of love that is willing to pay any price to achieve love's purpose was never broken.

I suggest therefore that there was never a moment when the *purpose* that generated unbroken vitality in the Father-Son relationship was revoked. If that is true, then we can envision that *the Spirit of their relationship was filling Jesus with the holy passion of the purpose that continued to unite the Father and the Son during that terrible season of lost intimacy.*

Was the Spirit filling Jesus with an awareness of the purpose He shared with the Father when Jesus lost all sense of enjoyed intimacy with His Father? Did Jesus therefore know the Spirit's fruit of joy as He relentlessly pursued His greatest purpose, to achieve what only suffering love could accomplish?

Is it possible, then, that we too, as Spirit-filled humans, can know the happiness of Jesus, the joy of the Spirit's fruit, to the degree that we are being formed to relate like Jesus, in the middle of great blessings or great trials, battling for a better love rather than for continued good times or relief from pain?

When we realize that the joy of advancing the purpose of God, of bringing God's relational kingdom of love into our community by putting Jesus-like love on display, even to those who hurt us deeply, is in fact first thing happiness, we will then be in position to battle for a better love. Spirit-filled disciples of Jesus will then know we are equipped and empowered to enter that battle, to love like Jesus even in our darkest moments, and to know the joy of pressing on toward our highest purpose: to enjoy God as our greatest good and to display Him by how we relate as our greatest privilege.

One Final Thought

In order for Jesus to experience the hell I deserve, He had to feel the reality of utterly lost intimacy with the Father. But because He experienced hell—not as a consequence He personally deserved but as a choice He made to be treated as I deserve to be treated—what He suffered during those three hours of lost intimacy with the Father is all the more worthy of worship.

Those who live in hell as relational beings without relationship are there by just consequence, not by free choice. Their prior choice to not trust Jesus to forgive their sins brought on the unanticipated and unwanted just consequence of hell. There is nothing praiseworthy about their suffering. It is deserved.

But the One who experienced hell by choice, to suffer what I deserved to suffer so that I could enjoy eternal intimacy with God, is all the more revealed as the revelation of the beauty of sacrificing, suffering love—the beauty we can display and enjoy as we battle for a better love.

Notes

Three Passages to Ponder As You Now Explore the Message of This Book

    1. Matthew 7:13–14 ESV; Isaiah 30:10–11; Psalms 32:8 ESV; 42:7–8.

Chapter 4 The One Prayer God Always Answers

    1. C. S. Lewis, *Mere Christianity* (New York: Macmillan, 1952), 173–74.

Chapter 5 Am I Even Interested in Praying the One Prayer God Always Answers?

    1. Dietrich Bonhoeffer, *The Cost of Discipleship* (New York: Simon and Schuster, 1995), 166.

Chapter 6 Our Deepest Hunger, Felt Most Deeply Only in Emptiness

    1. Iain Matthew, *The Impact of God* (London: Hodder and Stoughton, 1995), 135.

Chapter 7 Who Am I?

    1. As quoted in Claire Harman, *Robert Louis Stevenson: A Biography* (London: HarperCollins, 2005), 21.
    2. Robert Louis Stevenson, *Dr. Jekyll and Mr. Hyde* (New York: Random House, 1981), 64–65.
    3. Harman, *Robert Louis Stevenson*, 24.
    4. Stevenson, *Dr. Jekyll and Mr Hyde*, 82.
    5. Ibid., 84.

Chapter 8 A Passion for the Impossible

    1. Bonhoeffer, *Cost of Discipleship*, 131.
    2. Mark 10:27.

Chapter 9 Freedom to Follow

1. Jürgen Moltmann, *The Trinity and the Kingdom* (Minneapolis: Fortress Press, 1993), 217, 219.
2. Frederick Dale Brunner, *The Christbook: Matthew 1–12* (Grand Rapids: Eerdmans, 1987), 349.

Chapter 10 Three Faces of Entitlement

1. H. A. Ironside, *Expository Notes on the Gospel of Matthew* (New York: Loiseaux Brothers, Bible Truth Depot, 1948), 79.

Chapter 11 A Tale of Two Stories

1. Samuel Bolton, *The True Bounds of Christian Freedom* (Carlisle, PA: Banner of Truth Trust, 1964), 13.

Chapter 12 True or False?

1. C. S. Lewis, "Historicism," in *Christian Reflections* (Grand Rapids: Eerdmans, 1967), 106.

Chapter 13 Question 1: Who Is God?

1. John M. Frame, *The Doctrine of the Knowledge of God* (Phillipsburg, NJ: P & R, 1987), 9–10.
2. Ibid., 9.
3. This terribly brief and therefore inadequate answer to the question of "Who is God?" is richly explored in many books. Three stand out to me as accessibly written to every Christian: *Delighting in the Trinity* by Michael Reeves, *Experiencing the Trinity* by Darrell Johnson, and *The Great Dance* by Baxter Kruger. Two others are worth the required hard read: *The Social God and the Relational Self* by Stanley J. Grenz and *The Trinity and the Kingdom* by Jürgen Moltmann.
4. David Broughton Knox, *The Everlasting God* (Hertfordshire, England: Evangelical Press, 1982), 49, emphasis added.

Chapter 14 Question 2: What Is God Up To?

1. Lewis, *Mere Christianity*, 174–75.
2. Ibid., 76.

Chapter 15 Question 3: Who Are We?

1. As quoted in Iain Matthew, *Impact of God*, 17.
2. Michael Card, *Matthew: The Gospel of Identity* (Downers Grove, IL: InterVarsity, 2013), 71.
3. Thomas Chalmers, as quoted in Michael Reeves, *Delighting in the Trinity* (Downers Grove, IL: InterVarsity, 2012), 100.

Chapter 16 Question 4: What's Gone Wrong?

1. C. S. Lewis, *The Problem of Pain* (New York: Macmillan, 1966), 57.

2. Thomas Watson, *The Doctrine of Repentance* (Carlisle, PA: Banner of Truth Trust, 1987), 15.
3. Ibid., 9.
4. J. I. Packer, ed., *Puritan Papers*, vol. 2 (Phillipsburg, NJ: P & R, 2001), ix.
5. Ibid., 119, emphasis added.

Chapter 17 Question 5: What Has God Done about Our Problem?

1. As quoted in James Houston, *In Search of Happiness* (Batavia, IL: Lion Publishing, 1990), 53.
2. Ibid., 54.
3. Ibid., 189.
4. Ibid.
5. Ibid., 137.
6. Ibid., 135.

Chapter 18 Question 6: How Is the Spirit Working to Implement the Divine Solution to Our Human Problem?

1. As quoted in Iain Matthew, *Impact of God*, 26, 17, emphasis added.
2. Ibid., 25.
3. Ibid., 97.

Chapter 19 Question 7: How Can We Cooperate with the Spirit's Work?

1. As quoted in Malcolm Muggeridge, *Something Beautiful for God* (San Francisco: Harper & Row, 1971), 54.

Chapter 20 Engage the Battle

1. Penelope Wilcock, *The Hawk and the Dove* (Wheaton, IL: Crossway, 2000), 491.

Chapter 21 The Answer

1. Peter Kreeft, *Three Philosophies of Life* (San Francisco: Ignatius Press, 1989), 53.

Chapter 22 Life

1. Michael A. Eaton, *Ecclesiastes* (Downers Grove, IL: InterVarsity, 1983), 57.

Dr. Larry Crabb is a well-known psychologist, conference and seminar speaker, Bible teacher, popular author, and founder/director of NewWay Ministries. In addition to various other speaking and teaching opportunities, Dr. Crabb offers a weeklong School of Spiritual Direction held in Colorado Springs, CO, or Asheville, NC. He is currently Scholar in Residence at Colorado Christian University in Colorado and Visiting Professor for Richmont Graduate University in Georgia. In addition to producing several DVD teaching series, Dr. Crabb has authored many books, including *Fully Alive, Inside Out, Understanding People, The Marriage Builder, Finding God, Connecting, Becoming a True Spiritual Community, The Pressure's Off, Shattered Dreams, SoulTalk, The SoulCare Experience DVD, The PAPA Prayer, Real Church*, and *66 Love Letters*. Dr. Crabb and his wife, Rachael, live in the Denver area.

For additional information, please visit www.newwayministries.org.

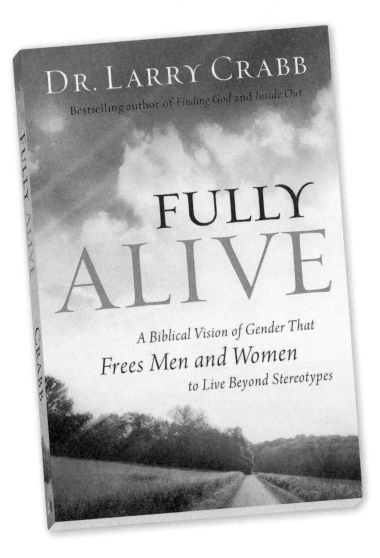

NEWWAY MINISTRIES WAS FORMED IN 2002 BY DR. LARRY CRABB.

It was birthed out of the passionate conviction that there is a new way to live made possible by the New Covenant that must become better known. We seek to introduce people to this new way of living, thinking, and relating that only the gospel makes possible. Our intended contribution to this revolution occurs through four distinct ministries:

- *Conferences*
- *School of Spiritual Direction*
- *Resource Library*
- *Internet Courses and Certification*

Dr. Crabb's work focuses on a biblical understanding of various aspects of life, such as marriage and manhood. Today, Larry is zeroing in on three topics:

- *Encounter*—what it means to experience God
- *Transformation*—what it takes to become like Christ
- *Community*—what real community is and how it helps us experience God and become spiritually formed

DR. LARRY CRABB is a psychologist, speaker, Bible teacher, bestselling author, and founder/director of **NewWay Ministries**

Our Calling - To ignite a revolution in relationships, a new way to live that explores the real battle in our souls and frees us to value intimacy with God more than blessings from God. It's a new way that's as old as the Bible. It's what following Jesus is all about.

Our Mission - To equip followers of Jesus to *enter the battle* for the souls of those they love—the battle to resist the Old Way and live the New Way.

www.newwayministries.org
info@newwayministries.org
phone: 970.262.9110
fax: 970.468.9696

Relevant. Intelligent. Engaging.